# Sabbath Dinner Cookbook 2

More vegetarian meal ideas for celebrating Sabbath with family and friends

JACQUELYN FAUCHER BECK
JEANNE BECK JARNES
KRISTEN JARNES

**Pacific Press® Publishing Association**
**Nampa, Idaho**
Oshawa, Ontario, Canada
www.pacificpress.com

Edited by: Bonnie Tyson-Flyn
Cover illustrations: © Getty Images
Cover and inside design: Michelle C. Petz

ISBN 0-8163-1910-3

# INTRODUCTION

How long has it been since you invited anyone over for Sabbath dinner? Were you afraid your house wasn't clean, you didn't have anything prepared to eat, and you just wanted to take a nap after eating, anyway? We'd like to challenge you to take a second look at the endless possibilities that exist when you take advantage of this special opportunity to be hospitable. Take a few extra minutes to plan something special for Sabbath dinner, and then invite someone else to share it with you! This book will help you in that endeavor.

We never cease to be amazed at all the delicious recipes that people share with us for these cookbooks! What a lot of good food there is! But there's a lot more to a recipe than just the ingredients. When you take the time to give of yourself in preparing a delicious meal and sharing it with friends, you have shared a little of the same spirit that is portrayed in the story of the widow's mite—our effort always multiplies when dedicated to the service of our Master!

Food is part of the tapestry that weaves through our lives and connects us to other people. So much of our culture and personal history comes through in these recipes that are submitted. You're getting more than just a menu—you're getting a little vignette into these people's lives and little peeks into the way others celebrate Sabbath. Many of these recipes have been carried around the globe and are just as satisfying in Greece as in India or the United States.

The first four menus in this cookbook feature the finalists from the Kellogg's® "Taste of Goodness" cook-off in Battle Creek, Michigan, on July 2, 2001. We were pleased that Jeanne was asked to be one of the cook-off judges, along with Susan Harvey, vice president of marketing for Pacific Press®. Congratulations to Audrey Child for being chosen as the winner, and kudos to the other three finalists and to all who took the time to submit their delicious recipes.

It's been fun putting this book together for you. Our thanks to everyone who shared their favorite menus. May you have many happy Sabbaths, and may God bless you all!

*Jackie*

*Kristen*

*Jeanne*

*(Note: Nutritional analysis was calculated with the Master Cook® software program. Results may vary depending on product used for the calculation.)*

# Sabbath Dinner Menu #1

*Contributed by Audrey Child of Spokane, Washington*

*Jeanne says:* Audrey won the recent Kellogg's® "Taste of Goodness" vegetarian cook-off with this casserole. In addition to the trip to Michigan and several days at the beautiful McCamly Plaza Hotel in Battle Creek, she won a year's supply ($1000 worth) of Worthington® and Loma Linda® products. Audrey has been married for forty-three years to Clayton Child, former youth director of Upper Columbia Conference. She is a registered nurse but is semi-retired and has a small typesetting business in their home. Her many interests include motorcycling, snowmobiling, skiing, boating, bicycling, music, camping, entertaining and, of course, cooking for her family and friends.

*Audrey says:* This recipe has been modified since I originally submitted it to Kellogg's® cook-off. I have notified the Kellogg kitchen that the day of the contest, I was so nervous I forgot to sauté the onions and celery! Yet it seems to me it tasted better than ever . . . so I have continued to make it that way!

Chicken Rice Casserole

Leafy Mandarin Salad

Fresh or frozen green peas

Whole-wheat dinner rolls
   with butter and jam

Ice cream strawberry sundaes

Sparkling cider

## Chicken Rice Casserole

*serves 8*

| PER SERVING | |
|---|---|
| CALORIES: | 355 |
| TOTAL FAT: | 13g |
| CHOLESTEROL: | 5mg |
| SODIUM: | 684mg |
| CARBOHYDRATE: | 47g |
| PROTEIN: | 11g |

2 cups cooked rice (white or brown)
1 cup finely chopped celery
1 cup finely chopped onions
1 10.75-ounce can low-fat condensed cream of mushroom soup, undiluted
1 8-ounce can water chestnuts, drained and sliced
1/2 cup light mayonnaise
2 12.5-ounce cans Worthington® FriChik®, drained and diced
1 teaspoon chickenlike seasoning and broth mix
2/3 cup crushed potato chips (optional)

Mix together all ingredients (except chips); place in an 8" x 8" x 2" (1 1/2-quart) glass baking dish coated with cooking spray. Sprinkle with potato chips. Bake at 350°F for 60 minutes.

## Leafy Mandarin Salad

*serves 6*

1 8-ounce can mandarin oranges, drained
1 ripe but firm avocado, peeled and sliced
6 to 8 cups torn salad greens

| PER SERVING | |
|---|---|
| CALORIES: | 16 |
| TOTAL FAT: | >1g |
| CHOLESTEROL: | 0mg |
| SODIUM: | 5mg |
| CARBOHYDRATE: | 4g |
| PROTEIN: | 1g |

Toss well and serve with Poppy-Seed Dressing.

## Poppy-Seed Dressing

*yields 2 cups (16 servings, 2 tablespoons each)*

1 cup light olive oil
$^1/_2$ cup red wine vinegar
1 teaspoon salt
$^1/_4$ cup granulated sugar
1 tablespoon dry mustard
1 tablespoon dehydrated onion
1 tablespoon poppy seeds

| PER SERVING | |
|---|---|
| CALORIES: | 138 |
| TOTAL FAT: | 14g |
| CHOLESTEROL: | 0mg |
| SODIUM: | 134mg |
| CARBOHYDRATE: | 4g |
| PROTEIN: | >1g |

In a blender combine oil, vinegar, salt, sugar, dry mustard, and onion. Cover; blend on low speed until ingredients are combined. Add poppy seeds; whir just to mix. Store, covered, in refrigerator up to one month. Bring to room temperature; shake well before serving.

**Pesto Alfredo Chicken and Broccoli Pasta**

**Tossed green salad**

**Sourdough bread dipped in garlic olive oil and balsamic vinegar**

**Dessert of choice**

# SABBATH DINNER MENU #2

*Contributed by Jim Pederson of Napa, California*

*Jeanne says:* Jim was the only male finalist in the Kellogg's® "Taste of Goodness" cook-off, and his pasta dish brought rave reviews from the judges! Jim is the secretary of the Northern California Conference of Seventh-day Adventists, and in his free time he enjoys traveling, music, and cooking. He concocted this dish one evening after arriving home from work hungry and in a hurry! Now it's one of his family's favorites and works well as a quick Sabbath dinner meal.

## Pesto Alfredo Chicken and Broccoli Pasta

*serves 8*

| PER SERVING | |
|---|---|
| CALORIES: | 496 |
| TOTAL FAT: | 32g |
| CHOLESTEROL: | 45mg |
| SODIUM: | 777mg |
| CARBOHYDRATE: | 34g |
| PROTEIN: | 21g |

8 ounces uncooked penne pasta
2 large crowns broccoli
1 12.5-ounce can Worthington® FriChik®
2 tablespoons olive oil
1 cup prepared basil pesto
1 16-ounce jar prepared alfredo sauce
1/2 cup grated Parmesan or Romano cheese

Cook pasta according to package directions. Drain and rinse.

Meanwhile, wash broccoli thoroughly; trim into florets. Drain *FriChik*®; cut into 1/4-inch slices.

Heat oil in a large nonstick fry pan. Add *FriChik*® and broccoli; sauté for 5 to 8 minutes, until broccoli is crispy-tender. Stir in pesto and alfredo sauce. Swirl a small amount of water in the jar; add to fry pan. Heat until bubbly, stirring frequently. Serve over hot pasta; top with grated Parmesan or Romano cheese.

**Cabbage Rolls**

**Mashed potatoes**

**Corn**

**Ice cream or pudding
(for the grandsons!)**

# SABBATH DINNER MENU #3

*Contributed by Lois Stephens of Shreveport, Louisiana*

*Jeanne says:* As one of the four finalists in the "Taste of Goodness" cook-off, Lois was accompanied to Battle Creek by her daughter and grandson (who promptly requested some Atlantis cereal for breakfast!). Lois tells me that she is very frugal about the amount of sodium she uses in cooking. Her husband Ray, until recently the Adventist Book Center Manager in the Arkansas/ Louisiana Conference, can rest easy, knowing his health is a priority with her!

## Cabbage Rolls

*serves 10*

1 large head green cabbage
1 19-ounce can Loma Linda® *Vege-Burger*®
2 14.5-ounce cans stewed tomatoes
1 cup long-grain rice
1 large onion, chopped
1/4 cup chopped green bell pepper
4 cloves garlic, minced or pressed
1/2 teaspoon onion powder

2 eggs
1/4 cup seasoned breadcrumbs
1/4 teaspoon sea salt
1 tablespoon brown beeflike seasoning
    and broth mix
2 10.75-ounce cans low-fat condensed
    tomato soup, undiluted

Cook head of cabbage in a large saucepan of boiling water for 10 to 15 minutes. Drain and let cool. Remove core; separate leaves.

Drain 1 can stewed tomatoes (reserve liquid); chop tomatoes. Mix *Vege-Burger*®, rice, onion, bell pepper, garlic, onion powder, eggs, breadcrumbs, salt, and chopped tomatoes (save liquid for later). Place about 1/4 cup filling in each cabbage leaf; wrap leaf around filling. Secure with a toothpick.

In a large saucepan, combine broth, tomato soup, remaining 1 can tomatoes (undrained), and two soup cans water (use reserved tomato liquid for part of the water measurement). Add cabbage rolls. Top with leftover raw cabbage, chopped, if desired. Cover; simmer over low heat for 60 to 90 minutes.

*Note: You can use 1/2 cup Morningstar Farms® Scramblers® in place of two eggs and eliminate the breadcrumbs. For a little more flavor, use Italian stewed tomatoes.*

| PER SERVING | |
| --- | --- |
| CALORIES: | 269 |
| TOTAL FAT: | 19g |
| CHOLESTEROL: | 37mg |
| SODIUM: | 1084mg |
| CARBOHYDRATE: | 41g |
| PROTEIN: | 15g |

**Jambalaya**

**Mango Salad**

**Fruit Salad**

**Whole-wheat rolls**

*Contributed by Altha Cleveland of Kirkland, Washington*

*Altha says:* I have been an Adventist since November of 1995. My husband has had a five-way bypass thanks to my (previously) rich cooking. Since we began watching 3ABN, I have learned so much from the health lectures. I realized that my husband's heart disease was a result of the way we ate. Little by little I have taken old favorite family recipes and changed them. Now that I don't use dairy products or anything that has a face, my husband's cholesterol has come down to 142, and his cardiologist can't believe the change.

As you can see, I am big on salads. This spinach salad recipe is a hit at any potluck. Every time someone tastes the salad for the first time, he or she asks for the recipe. It is great with any meal or may be used as a light meal, served by itself with whole-wheat rolls and fresh fruit. The fruit salad was a special treat that was always on Grandmother McFarland's table at Christmas family gatherings. It makes a light and nutritious dessert.

## Jambalaya

*serves 8*

2 tablespoons olive oil, divided
1 cup chopped onions
1/2 cup chopped celery
1 teaspoon minced or pressed garlic
1 28-ounce can peeled whole tomatoes
1 teaspoon gumbo filé powder
1 teaspoon salt
1 teaspoon liquid pepper sauce

1 tablespoon chopped fresh parsley
1 16-ounce package frozen cut okra
2 cups vegetable broth
1 8-ounce package Morningstar Farms®
    Breakfast Links® or Worthington® *Prosage*
    *Links*®, cut into 1-inch pieces
12 ounces extra-firm tofu, frozen then thawed
4 cups cooked brown rice

Heat 1 tablespoon oil in a large saucepan. Add onion, celery, and garlic. Sauté over medium heat 5 minutes or until vegetables begin to soften. Add tomatoes; break apart with a spoon. Stir in gumbo filé powder, salt, pepper sauce, parsley, okra, and broth. Cover; simmer 20 minutes.

Squeeze as much liquid as possible from thawed tofu without crushing the block. *It will have a "spongy" texture and may tend to crumble.* Cut into 1/2-inch cubes.

Spray a large frying pan with cooking spray; heat 1 tablespoon oil. Add tofu; brown on one side. Spray tofu with cooking spray; turn pieces over to brown the other side. *(You can sprinkle the tofu with a little more gumbo filé powder for additional flavor.)* Remove tofu from skillet; add to tomato mixture. Add links to skillet; sauté over medium-high heat for 5 minutes or until lightly browned. Add links to tomato mixture; simmer for 5 to 10 minutes. Adjust seasonings. Serve over hot cooked brown rice.

*Note: Cook raw brown rice in a dry skillet for a few minutes before adding water. Stir constantly—do not let it brown. This makes cooked rice fluffier.*

| PER SERVING | |
| --- | --- |
| CALORIES: | 330 |
| TOTAL FAT: | 13g |
| CHOLESTEROL: | 1mg |
| SODIUM: | 946mg |
| CARBOHYDRATE: | 44g |
| PROTEIN: | 14g |

## Mango Salad

*serves 6 to 8*

1 bunch red leaf lettuce
1 or 2 mangos, cubed
1/4 to 1/2 cup unsweetened shredded coconut
Juice of one lime
1 tablespoon sugar (or 1 to 2 packets sugar substitute)
1/4 cup Best Foods® *Citrus Splash*® dressing

Wash lettuce; tear into bite-size pieces. Slice cheeks of mangos, score into cubes, then push the curve inside-out so the cubes can be sliced off the skin. Peel the seed portion; slice off fruit; cube. Add mango and coconut to prepared red lettuce. Combine lime juice, sugar, and dressing; add to salad just before serving.

*Note: This salad looks pretty served on individual salad plates.*

## Fruit Salad

*serves 8 to 10*

1 cup large-size pearl tapioca
1 cup sugar
1 large package frozen strawberries
1 large can crushed pineapple
2 Red Delicious apples, unpeeled, diced
3 oranges, peeled, membrane removed
   (I use canned mandarin oranges, drained well)
3 bananas, sliced
1 cup halved red seedless grapes
1/2 to 1 cup chopped walnuts or pecans
1 8-ounce container light whipped topping (optional)

| PER SERVING | |
| --- | --- |
| CALORIES: | 365 |
| TOTAL FAT: | 10g |
| CHOLESTEROL: | 0mg |
| SODIUM: | 8mg |
| CARBOHYDRATE: | 71g |
| PROTEIN: | 3g |

Soak tapioca overnight in 3 cups water. *Do not drain.* Pour into a medium saucepan, add one or two cups water. Add sugar; bring to a boil, stirring frequently for about 30 minutes or until tapioca is translucent. Set aside for 2 to 5 minutes. Stir in frozen strawberries; let cool. Add diced apple. Stir in oranges, bananas, grapes, and nuts. Cool in refrigerator. Serve with or without whipped topping. *(My grandmother used real whipped cream!)*

**Mock Salmon Loaf**

**Pecan-Crusted Squash**

**Herbed Scalloped Tomatoes**

*Greek salad*

*Dinner rolls*

*Favorite berry cobbler
    with cream*

# S A B B A T H   D I N N E R   M E N U   # 5

*Contributed by Diane Matson of College Place, Washington*

*Jackie says:* Diane is an excellent cook; she loves people and enjoys having company. She works closely with her husband Neal, one of the pastors of the Village Church in College Place, Washington, in visiting the church members and caring for their needs.

*Diane says:* This menu of casseroles is nice because they can all be prepared on Friday. On Sabbath morning before leaving for church, put the Herbed Scalloped Tomatoes in the oven and set the timer to start baking 45 minutes before time to serve Sabbath dinner. Set the other two casseroles out on the counter, ready to put in the oven when you get home from church.

While preparing lunch, pop the other two casseroles into the oven about 30 minutes before serving so everything is hot and ready to put on the table at the same time. I like to keep in mind that "serving guests with love, reminds them of the One above."

## Mock Salmon Loaf

*serves 8*

24 ounces of frozen Worthington® *Chicken Style Soymeat®*
1 4-ounce can Tartex® vegetable pâté
1 medium onion, minced
1 large stalk celery, minced
2 eggs, beaten or 1/2 cup Morningstar Farms® *Scramblers®*
1/2 cup Miracle Whip® salad dressing
1/2 teaspoon paprika
1/2 cup dry breadcrumbs

| PER SERVING | |
| --- | --- |
| CALORIES: | 238 |
| TOTAL FAT: | 14g |
| CHOLESTEROL: | 52mg |
| SODIUM: | 774mg |
| CARBOHYDRATE: | 11g |
| PROTEIN: | 17g |

Grind soymeat. Combine all ingredients; mix well. (Since Tartex® is a stiff paste, mash a small amount with several tablespoons of the rest of the mixture. Continue until Tartex® is blended.) Press mixture into a flat baking dish. Bake at 325°F for 60 minutes or until done. *Cover during the first half of the baking time.* Serve with tartar sauce or a white sauce, garnished with parsley.

*Note: This casserole can be baked on Friday and warmed up on Sabbath morning. Take it out of the refrigerator Sabbath morning and set it on the counter. Place in oven with the other casseroles 25 to 30 minutes before serving, so that it is piping hot.*

## Pecan-Crusted Squash

*serves 8*

2 pounds cooked and mashed
    yellow winter squash
6 tablespoons butter or margarine
4 tablespoons cream
4 tablespoons brown sugar
1/2 teaspoon salt
1/4 teaspoon nutmeg
1/4 teaspoon ginger
1 cup chopped pecans

**Topping**
1/2 cup chopped pecans
6 tablespoons white corn syrup
4 tablespoons brown sugar
2 tablespoons butter or margarine,
    melted

| PER SERVING | |
| --- | --- |
| CALORIES: | 389 |
| TOTAL FAT: | 28g |
| CHOLESTEROL: | 7mg |
| SODIUM: | 295mg |
| CARBOHYDRATE: | 36g |
| PROTEIN: | 3g |

Combine squash ingredients; place in a buttered casserole.

Combine TOPPING ingredients. Drizzle over squash mixture. Bake at 350°F for 20 to 25 minutes or until a crust is formed.

*Friday preparation:* Make the squash mixture; don't add the chopped pecans.

*On Sabbath:* Add 1 cup chopped pecans to squash mixture. Prepare topping; drizzle it over the squash just before baking.

## Herbed Scalloped Tomatoes

*serves 8*

4 cups canned tomatoes, diced
2 1/2 cups herbed stuffing mix, divided
1 small onion, chopped
2 tablespoons sugar
1/2 teaspoon salt
1/2 teaspoon nutmeg
1/2 teaspoon leaf oregano, crumbled
1/4 teaspoon leaf rosemary, crumbled
1/4 cup butter or margarine

| PER SERVING | |
| --- | --- |
| CALORIES: | 125 |
| TOTAL FAT: | 6g |
| CHOLESTEROL: | >1mg |
| SODIUM: | 627mg |
| CARBOHYDRATE: | 16g |
| PROTEIN: | 3g |

In a buttered 2-quart casserole, mix together tomatoes and two cups stuffing mix. Stir in onion, sugar, and seasonings; dot with butter or margarine. Sprinkle remaining stuffing mix on top. Bake at 375°F for 45 minutes.

**Holiday Roast**

**Broiled Apple Rings**

**Sautéed New Potatoes With Rosemary**

*Fresh steamed broccoli*

*Whole-wheat rolls*

**Tropical Punch**

**Hot Fudge Sauce**
   *with vanilla frozen yogurt*

# S A B B A T H   D I N N E R   M E N U   # 6

*Contributed by Susan Harvey of Boise, Idaho*

*Susan says:* The Holiday Roast recipe is adapted from one found in volume 3 of *Vegetarian Cookery,* a 5-volume cookbook set published by Pacific Press in 1971. It has been our family's favorite for Christmas and other special occasions for many years. The leftovers make great sandwiches.

## Holiday Roast

*serves 8*

| PER SERVING | |
| --- | --- |
| CALORIES: | 410 |
| TOTAL FAT: | 50g |
| CHOLESTEROL: | 70mg |
| SODIUM: | 1504mg |
| CARBOHYDRATE: | 22g |
| PROTEIN: | 22g |

1/2 cup margarine
2 medium onions, chopped fine
2 cloves garlic, minced or pressed
1 cup finely chopped fresh mushrooms
1 20-ounce can + 1 cup Loma Linda® *Vege-Burger*®
2 packets brown beeflike seasoning and broth mix
1/4 cup hot water
1 cup finely chopped pecans
3 eggs, beaten or 3/4 cup Morningstar Farms® *Scramblers*®
1/2 cup breading meal
1/2 cup bread crumbs
1/2 teaspoon salt
2 teaspoons poultry seasoning
3 bay leaves

Heat oven to 350°F. In a large skillet, sauté onions, garlic, and mushrooms in margarine. Add *Vege-Burger*®; braise slightly. Dissolve beeflike seasoning in hot water; combine with all other ingredients in a large bowl. Spray a 9" x 5" x 2 3/4" loaf pan with cooking spray; line with aluminum foil, leaving enough foil to fold over roast. Spray foil with cooking spray. Turn roast mixture into pan; place three bay leaves on top. Fold foil over top. Bake 75 minutes, until set. Refrigerate.

Reheat at 300°F for 20 minutes. To serve, remove bay leaves; carefully turn roast out onto plate or platter. Surround and garnish with Broiled Apple Rings (see p. 22) and fresh parsley.

## Broiled Apple Rings

*serves 8*

3 large Granny Smith apples (or any tart apples)
6 tablespoons butter or margarine, melted
3 tablespoons lemon juice
3 tablespoons granulated sugar
1/2 teaspoon cinnamon

| PER SERVING | |
|---|---|
| CALORIES: | 127 |
| TOTAL FAT: | 9g |
| CHOLESTEROL: | 0mg |
| SODIUM: | 100mg |
| CARBOHYDRATE: | 13g |
| PROTEIN: | >1g |

Wash and core apples. *(Leave peel on or remove, as you prefer. Apples will hold together better with peel left on.)* Slice apples into 1/4-inch-thick rings; arrange in a shallow pan or cookie sheet sprayed with cooking spray. Mix melted butter and lemon juice. Mix sugar and cinnamon, set aside. Brush butter-and-lemon-juice mixture generously onto apple rings. Broil 4 to 5 minutes, or until slices begin to soften. Turn with a spatula. Brush second side with butter and lemon juice; sprinkle with cinnamon and sugar. Broil 3 to 5 additional minutes, or until golden brown. *(Can be prepared ahead of time and re-warmed on cookie sheet in oven just before serving.)*

## Tropical Punch

Mix together equal parts limeade, white grape juice, and ginger ale.

## Sautéed New Potatoes With Rosemary

*serves 8*

1 1/2 to 2 pounds small red potatoes, scrubbed
3 tablespoons olive oil
2 tablespoons chopped fresh or 2 teaspoons dried, crushed rosemary
Salt to taste

| PER SERVING | |
| --- | --- |
| CALORIES: | 135 |
| TOTAL FAT: | 5g |
| CHOLESTEROL: | 0mg |
| SODIUM: | 273mg |
| CARBOHYDRATE: | 20g |
| PROTEIN: | 2g |

*Friday preparation:* Boil potatoes, unpeeled, until just tender. Drain, cool, and refrigerate.

*On Sabbath:* Cut potatoes into halves or quarters, according to their size. Heat olive oil in skillet; add potatoes, chopped rosemary, and salt to taste. Cook, turning occasionally, until potatoes are golden brown. Turn into a serving dish.

## Hot Fudge Sauce

1 12-ounce can low fat sweetened condensed milk
2 squares unsweetened baking chocolate

| PER SERVING | |
| --- | --- |
| CALORIES: | 160 |
| TOTAL FAT: | 7g |
| CHOLESTEROL: | 13mg |
| SODIUM: | 0mg |
| CARBOHYDRATE: | 23g |
| PROTEIN: | 4g |

In the microwave or a double boiler, melt chocolate in condensed milk, whisking occasionally to blend. Serve hot over vanilla frozen yogurt.

**Beth's Rice Entree**

**Mandarin Salad**

**Fresh broccoli**

**Crescent rolls or dinner rolls**

**Cream pie**

**Guava/Cranraspberry Punch**

# Sabbath Dinner Menu #7

*Contributed by Beth Burgess Miracle of Auburn, California*

*Jeanne says:* Beth and I have been friends since we were little girls, when our parents were missionaries in Sri Lanka (Ceylon at the time). Later, we had the good fortune of living about a mile away from each other for several years here in Idaho—before she and her family recently moved to California. She can whip up a delicious meal with little effort (to all appearances!), much to the delight of her husband, Mike, and son and daughter, Mark and Michelle.

*Beth says:* This entree is not in print anywhere because I created it! Note that it can also be heated in the microwave for a quick and easy meal during the week. I just add a side of cottage cheese and fruit, and we've got dinner in a jiffy!

One day my husband Mike came home raving about a salad one of his employees had brought to work. He liked it so much that he had even asked for the recipe! I figured if it was that good, I'd better check it out. After making the salad, I could see why he enjoyed it so much, and it has been a favorite with our guests ever since.

## Beth's Rice Entree

*serves 12*

| PER SERVING | |
|---|---|
| CALORIES: | 271 |
| TOTAL FAT: | 4g |
| CHOLESTEROL: | 8mg |
| SODIUM: | 879mg |
| CARBOHYDRATE: | 47g |
| PROTEIN: | 11g |

4 cups instant rice
2 10.75-ounce cans low-fat condensed cream of mushroom soup, undiluted
2 cups light sour cream
1/4 cup finely chopped onion
1/2 cup finely chopped celery
1/4 to 1/2 cup soy sauce
1 20-ounce can grated Worthington® *Skallops*® or any similar meat substitute

Cook instant rice according to package directions; transfer to a large bowl. Stir together mushroom soup and sour cream; add to rice. Sauté chopped onion and celery in a frying pan with water, not oil. When cooked, add to soup-rice mixture.

Fry *Skallops*® in soy sauce until sauce has been absorbed into the meat and the meat is tender. Add *Skallops*® to rice; stir. Place rice mixture in a casserole; heat at 350°F for 30 to 45 minutes.

*Beth says:* I have noticed that the meat substitute, having been fried in soy sauce, is very tender and gives the casserole an excellent flavor. I also use this method for adding vegemeat to boxed casseroles that call for tuna, and the result is marvelous.

## Mandarin Salad

*serves 8*

**Sugared almonds**

1/2 cup sliced almonds
2 tablespoons + 2 teaspoons sugar

**Salad**

1/4 head iceberg lettuce,
    torn into bite-size pieces
1/2 bunch romaine lettuce,
    torn into bite-size pieces
2 medium stalks celery, chopped
4 green onions with tops, thinly sliced
Sweet-Sour Dressing (recipe follows)
2 11-ounce cans mandarin oranges, drained

Cook almonds and sugar over low heat, stirring constantly, until sugar is melted and almonds are coated. Cool; break apart. Store at room temperature.

Place lettuces in a plastic bag; add celery and onions. *Just* before you are ready to serve, pour Sweet-Sour Dressing into bag; add orange segments. Close bag tightly; shake until salad greens and orange segments are well coated. Add almonds; shake. Serve *immediately*.

*Do-ahead tips:* You can make the sugared almonds in advance, and before the dressing is added, you can place the salad greens in a tightly-closed bag and refrigerate up to 24 hours ahead.

| PER SERVING | |
|---|---|
| CALORIES: | 172 |
| TOTAL FAT: | 12g |
| CHOLESTEROL: | 0mg |
| SODIUM: | 150mg |
| CARBOHYDRATE: | 17g |
| PROTEIN: | 3g |

## Sweet-Sour Dressing

1/4 cup vegetable oil
2 tablespoons sugar
2 tablespoons vinegar
2 tablespoons snipped fresh parsley
1/2 teaspoon salt
10 shakes of red pepper sauce

Shake all ingredients in tightly covered jar; use immediately.

## Beth's Pie Crust

*for an 8- or 9-inch, one-crust pie*

*Beth says:* Once I was preparing food for a Christmas party, and my girlfriend volunteered to help by making the piecrusts. Believing that a pie is only as good as its crust, I cautiously asked what ingredients she used. Much to my amazement and relief, I found she uses the same recipe as I do! Here it is: a piecrust that is flaky and tender every time.

1 cup white flour
$1/4$ teaspoon salt
$1/3$ cup + 1 tablespoon shortening
2 tablespoons + 1 teaspoon water

*Tip:* Press firmly around edges of pie tin so crust doesn't "shrink" when baking, prick the bottom and sides generously with a fork, and sprinkle dried beans (any kind) on the bottom to keep bubbles from forming. Bake at 475°F for 8 to 10 minutes. Just scoop out the beans and throw them away, cool the crust, add your favorite cream pie filling—and you've got a delicious desert.

## Guava/ Cranraspberry Punch

Combine equal parts chilled cranraspberry juice, chilled guava juice, and half-again as much chilled lemon-lime soda of your choice.

**Savory Wild Rice**

**Creamed FriChik**

**Green beans (fresh or frozen) with toasted almonds**

**Veg plate: Tomato slices sprinkled with basil, carrot sticks, olives, and pickles**

**Breadsticks**

**White grape-peach juice**

**Berry Pudding Cake**

# SABBATH DINNER MENU #8

*Contributed by Carol Dodge of Meridian, Idaho*

*Carol says:* I got the special Savory Wild Rice recipe from my friend Mary Johnson (Alaska Conference first lady) on my first trip to Alaska. It's fun to collect recipes from friends so you can remember them when you make their recipes. The Pudding Cake recipe is a favorite of mine. I really enjoy baking, cooking, and collecting cookbooks and recipes. My interest right now is regional cookbooks. When we travel I like to take along a cookbook to "read" and mark recipes to try. My husband teases me about never serving the same thing twice. Sometimes he'll say, "Didn't we have this ten years ago?"

## Savory Wild Rice

*serves 8*

1 cup uncooked wild rice
3 eggs or 8 ounces tofu*
2 tablespoons margarine
1/2 cup sliced green onions
1 cup sliced celery
1 cup sliced mushrooms

2 4-ounce cans water chestnuts, chopped
2 teaspoons beeflike seasoning and broth mix
1/2 teaspoon salt
1/2 cup chopped fresh parsley
   or 1/4 cup dried parsley flakes

| PER SERVING | |
|---|---|
| CALORIES: | 133 |
| TOTAL FAT: | 5g |
| CHOLESTEROL: | 70mg |
| SODIUM: | 367mg |
| CARBOHYDRATE: | 18g |
| PROTEIN: | 6g |

Preheat oven to 350°F. Cook rice according to package directions. Scramble egg in margarine until golden brown; use a slotted spoon to break into small pieces. Remove from skillet. Sauté onions, celery, and mushrooms until tender. Add all other ingredients; place in a 9" x 13" casserole. Cover with foil; heat for 30 minutes.

*Note: If using tofu, freeze it first, then thaw and squeeze out liquid for a chewier texture. Crumble and scramble as you would eggs. Substituting tofu for eggs reduces the cholesterol content to 0mg per serving.*

## Creamed FriChik

*serves 8*

| PER SERVING | |
|---|---|
| CALORIES: | 206 |
| TOTAL FAT: | 13g |
| CHOLESTEROL: | 9mg |
| SODIUM: | 663mg |
| CARBOHYDRATE: | 11g |
| PROTEIN: | 11g |

1/4 cup margarine or butter
1/4 cup flour
1 teaspoon salt
4 cups 2% milk
2 12.5-ounce cans Worthington® FriChik®, drained, chopped, and fried or baked until crispy
1 medium onion, chopped, sautéed until tender

Melt margarine. Remove from heat; stir in flour and salt. Blend well; then add milk. Return to medium heat; stir constantly until the sauce is somewhat thickened. Add chicken and onion; serve over Savory Wild Rice (see p. 29).

*Variation:* Use this recipe to make creamed peas; add the chicken to the Savory Wild Rice recipe. Or add peas to the creamed FriChik.

## Berry Pudding Cake

*serves 8*

1 1/2 cups blueberries, thawed if frozen
1 1/2 cups raspberries, thawed if frozen
1 cup flour
1 teaspoon baking powder
1/4 teaspoon salt
1 1/2 cups sugar, divided
1/2 cup 2% milk
3 tablespoons unsalted butter, melted
1 teaspoon vanilla
1 tablespoon cornstarch
1 cup boiling water

| PER SERVING | |
| --- | --- |
| CALORIES: | 280 |
| TOTAL FAT: | 5g |
| CHOLESTEROL: | 13mg |
| SODIUM: | 138mg |
| CARBOHYDRATE: | 58g |
| PROTEIN: | 3g |

Preheat oven to 350°F. Place fruit in the bottom of a buttered 9" x 9" or 10-inch round cake pan or baking dish. Combine flour, baking powder, salt, and 3/4 cup sugar in a mixing bowl. Add milk, butter, and vanilla. Using an electric mixer, beat until smooth. Spread batter over fruit. Combine remaining 3/4 cup sugar and cornstarch; sprinkle over batter. Pour boiling water over mixture. Bake 45 minutes or until tester comes out clean when inserted in center. Serve with cream, vanilla frozen yogurt, ice cream, or whipped topping.

**Chicken a la King**

**California Salad**

**Spinach With Cream Sauce**

**Assorted relishes**

**Dinner rolls**

**Instant Orange Mousse**

**White grape juice with ginger ale**

# SABBATH DINNER MENU #9

*Contributed by Carla Baker of Keene, Texas*

*Jeanne says:* Carla is the Women's Ministries Director for the Southwestern Union Conference. Although her schedule is busy, she can always find time for real Southern hospitality. It was heartwarming to learn that she and my maternal grandmother, Donita Teague, worked together on the church bulletin when they were both members of the Oak Cliff church in Dallas, Texas. Carla would type the bulletin and get it printed, then take it to Donita, who would affix the mailing labels and write little notes of encouragement to inactive or ill members. Grandmother passed away three years ago, but her memory lives on in our hearts—and in Carla's.

*Carla says:* This Chicken a la King recipe is different and very quick to prepare. It makes an elegant-looking entree because it's served in puffed pastry shells. It's been my son's favorite Sabbath entree since he was six, and even though he's grown now, he still requests it when he comes home for a visit. The California Salad is a very special tossed salad with some unusual ingredients. It's always a hit with my guests and is my son's all-time favorite salad. The Instant Orange Mousse is quick and light and is a good way to end a typically heavy Sabbath dinner. I make it just before I serve dinner, spoon it into individual sherbet dishes, and put them in the freezer until time to serve dessert.

## Chicken a la King

*serves 8*

3 eggs
3 tablespoons minced green onions
1 can fat-free Worthington® *Diced Chik*®
1 can sliced mushrooms
1 10.75-ounce can low-fat condensed cream of mushroom soup, undiluted
1 cup light sour cream
$1/2$ to 1 cup 2% milk (add a little at a time)
1 teaspoon chickenlike seasoning and broth mix
8 puff pastry shells

| PER SERVING | |
| --- | --- |
| CALORIES: | 378 |
| TOTAL FAT: | 22g |
| CHOLESTEROL: | 78mg |
| SODIUM: | 651mg |
| CARBOHYDRATE: | 30g |
| PROTEIN: | 12g |

In a skillet, scramble eggs. As the eggs are beginning to set, add onions, *Diced Chik*®, and mushrooms. Stir in soup, sour cream, milk, and seasoning (mixture should not be too thin). Cook together until mixture is thoroughly heated and bubbling.

Cook pastry shells according to package directions; remove centers. Fill with Chicken a la King. Serve on an attractive platter.

## California Salad

*serves 8*

8 to 10 cups torn lettuce (use 3 or 4 different kinds)
3/4 cup coconut
1 cup dried apricots, chopped
1/2 cup salted sunflower seeds
1/2 cup toasted slivered almonds
3 or 4 green onions, sliced

**Dressing**
1/2 cup sugar
1 teaspoon dried mustard
1 teaspoon salt
1/3 cup white vinegar or lemon juice
3/4 cup canola oil

| PER SERVING | |
|---|---|
| CALORIES: | 422 |
| TOTAL FAT: | 32g |
| CHOLESTEROL: | 0mg |
| SODIUM: | 295mg |
| CARBOHYDRATE: | 33g |
| PROTEIN: | 6g |

DRESSING: Put sugar, dried mustard, and salt in a food processor. Pour vinegar or lemon juice over dry ingredients: process, using knife blade. Add oil slowly through chute while processor is running. Process until smooth and sugar is dissolved.

## Spinach With Cream Sauce

*serves 8*

| PER | SERVING | |
|---|---|---|
| CALORIES: | 145 | |
| TOTAL FAT: | 12g | |
| CHOLESTEROL: | 20mg | |
| SODIUM: | 409mg | |
| CARBOHYDRATE: | 8g | |
| PROTEIN: | 3g | |

Cook 2 packages frozen spinach according to package directions. Drain well; place in a serving bowl. *You can substitute any green vegetable.* Pour Cream Sauce (recipe follows) over top while spinach is warm, keeping sauce in the center of the dish and leaving sides uncovered.

## Cream Sauce

1 cup 2% milk
2 tablespoons butter or margarine
2 tablespoons flour

1/2 to 1 teaspoon seasoned salt
1 cup light mayonnaise

Cook milk, butter, flour, and salt in a saucepan until thickened and bubbling. Remove from heat; stir in mayonnaise.

## Instant Orange Mousse

*serves 4*

2/3 cup hot water
2 packets unflavored gelatin
1/2 cup sugar
2 tablespoons whipping cream

1 6-ounce can frozen orange juice
   concentrate
1/2 teaspoon vanilla
2 cups ice cubes

| PER | SERVING | |
|---|---|---|
| CALORIES: | 353 | |
| TOTAL FAT: | 3g | |
| CHOLESTEROL: | 10mg | |
| SODIUM: | 112mg | |
| CARBOHYDRATE: | 80g | |
| PROTEIN: | 4g | |

Process hot water and gelatin in food processor for 30 seconds. Add sugar; process 5 seconds. Add cream, juice, and vanilla; add ice cubes a few at a time. Process until very smooth. Spoon into 4 sherbet dishes; serve immediately or store in freezer up to 1/2 hour before serving.

**Pecan Patties**

**Mashed potatoes**

**Cooked vegetable of choice**

**Fresh veggies**

**Garlic bread**

**Apple or pumpkin pie**

**White grape juice
    with ginger ale**

# S ABBATH  D INNER  M ENU  # 1 0

*Contributed by Eve Rusk of Caldwell, Idaho*

*Jeanne says:* Eve works as the administrative assistant for the officers of the Idaho Conference in Boise. Her husband Terry is a valuable part of the ISS team at Pacific Press. Eve is a talented gal with many interests, including cross-stitch, playing the piano, and singing. She is always willing to help out at church in any way she can, whether that means serving as head elder, Sabbath School teacher, praise-team leader, worship coordinator, or choir director. Oh that all churches could have members as versatile and willing as Eve! Her husband and sons, Ted and Keith, love these man-sized pecan patties—and I do too!

*Eve says:* This is based on a recipe that my eighth-grade teacher, Linda Worth, gave to my mom. It has become a family favorite. We will often serve it at Christmas. It also is a great one for Sabbath—it cooks while you are at church!

## Pecan Patties

*makes 12 patties*

1 cup pecan meal or 1 cup whole pecans ground in a food processor or blender
1 cup quick oatmeal
1 small onion, diced
1 1/2 cups  Morningstar Farms® *Scramblers®* or 1 1/2 cups soft tofu, whipped
1 cup shredded cheddar cheese or tofu cheddar cheese
Tomato Sauce (recipe follows)

Combine and mix ingredients (except Tomato Sauce). Use a scant 1/3 cup measure to make patties. Drop into a nonstick fry pan sprayed with olive oil; flatten with a spatula. Brown on both sides over medium-low to medium heat (about 5 minutes first side, 3 to 4 second side). *Spray pan with olive oil before frying each batch.* Prepare Tomato Sauce *(or use store-bought spaghetti sauce).*

Pour a layer of Tomato Sauce into a crockpot; add a layer of patties. Cover with sauce. *Repeat until all patties are in crockpot. Make sure the top patties are covered with sauce.* Cook on low, covered, for 3 to 4 hours.

*Note: The patties make great sandwiches when cold. Slice each patty into two patties.*

| PER SERVING | |
|---|---|
| CALORIES: | 146 |
| TOTAL FAT: | 8g |
| CHOLESTEROL: | 10mg |
| SODIUM: | 516mg |
| CARBOHYDRATE: | 12g |
| PROTEIN: | 7g |

## Tomato Sauce

1 29-ounce can tomato sauce
1 teaspoon dried oregano
1 garlic clove, crushed
Salt to taste

**Pasta-Link Dish**

**Green vegetable or salad of choice**

**Bread or rolls**

# SABBATH DINNER MENU #11

*Contributed by Jill Johnson of Freeport, Maine*

*Jeanne says:* Jill works at the Northern New England Adventist Book Center. She has been married for 25 years to her husband Alaric, now retired from military service. Their son Andrew attends Pine Tree Academy.

*Jill says:* Our family has a very busy schedule, so I am always looking for quick and easy one-dish recipes for dinner. This particular dish can be served as a one-dish meal with your favorite breads, but you can also include a salad on the side if you wish. I got this recipe from my older brother, and it has always been a favorite for our family. What a great way to get your kids to eat a vegetable—combine it with their favorite hot dog!

## Pasta-Link Dish

*serves 8*

| PER SERVING | |
|---|---|
| CALORIES: | 330 |
| TOTAL FAT: | 10g |
| CHOLESTEROL: | 4mg |
| SODIUM: | 781mg |
| CARBOHYDRATE: | 43g |
| PROTEIN: | 17g |

1 14-ounce package angel hair pasta
1 small head cabbage, shredded
1 small onion, chopped
1 or 2 cloves (to taste) garlic, minced
3/4 cup chopped fresh parsley (amount can vary to your liking)
1 to 2 tablespoons chickenlike seasoning and broth mix
1 tablespoon olive oil
Turmeric (optional; will add a little color and different flavor)
1 can Loma Linda® *Linketts®* or your favorite vegetarian hot dog
Parmesan cheese

Break pasta in half; cook as directed. Drain and set aside.

Cook cabbage and onion with a little water in a 4-quart saucepan. When tender, add garlic, parsley, chickenlike seasoning, olive oil, and other optional seasonings. Mix well; add *Linketts®*. Stir and add pasta. Toss well, turn out into a serving dish, and sprinkle with Parmesan cheese. *This is a great quick one-dish meal served with your favorite garlic bread or rolls.*

**Nancy's Chicken Potpie**

**Tossed salad**

**Dinner rolls**

**Iced Apple Cake**

# Sabbath Dinner Menu #12

*Contributed by Holly Beck of Lincoln, Nebraska*

*Jeanne says:* Holly is married to my cousin, Bob, and as you can see from her comments below, she's a dynamo of a gal! Her home is always open to Union College students and anyone else who she perceives might need a little nurturing. Her quick wit, sense of humor, and laid-back attitude immediately put guests at ease.

*Holly says:* Every month I cook for our Women's Ministry Group, "Women in Touch." We always cook for 325 women, and it is fun to come up with new recipes. We also have frequent potlucks with friends, and everyone shares their recipes! I like to keep things simple, so with this potpie, I often just serve a regular tossed salad and dinner rolls. Not especially creative—but delicious and easy!

## Nancy's Chicken Potpie

*serves 8*

2 cups diced raw potatoes
1 cup bite-size carrot pieces
1 small onion, chopped
1/2 cup frozen corn
1/2 cup frozen peas
1 12.5-ounce can Worthington® FriChik®,
    cut into bite-size pieces (reserve liquid)

**Sauce**

2 cups plain soymilk (I like the Silk® brand)
3 tablespoons flour

Reserved liquid from Worthington® FriChik®
1 envelope of G Washington's® seasoning
Chickenlike seasoning and broth mix,
    to taste

**Crust**

2 cups flour
1/4 cup wheat germ
1 teaspoon salt
1/2 cup oil
1/2 cup boiling water

| PER SERVING | |
| --- | --- |
| CALORIES: | 373 |
| TOTAL FAT: | 18g |
| CHOLESTEROL: | 0mg |
| SODIUM: | 428mg |
| CARBOHYDRATE: | 42g |
| PROTEIN: | 11g |

Boil potatoes, carrots, and onions in just enough water to cover until tender. Drain. In the meantime, prepare cream sauce.

Cook SAUCE ingredients over medium heat, stirring continuously until thickened. *Add a little milk if sauce seems too thick.* Add potatoes, carrots, onions, peas, corn, and *FriChik®. You can also add other vegetables to your liking!* Pour into lightly greased 9" x 13" baking dish.

CRUST: Mix together flour, wheat germ, and salt; add oil and water. Form a ball; then roll out between wax paper to approximately a 9" x 13" size. Place on top of filling. Bake at 350°F until bubbly and crust is browned.

## Iced Apple Cake

*serves 18*

### Cake

3 eggs
1 cup oil
2 cups sugar
2 cups flour
2 teaspoons cinnamon
1 teaspoon baking soda
1/2 teaspoon salt
1 teaspoon vanilla
4 cups peeled, chopped apples (I use Granny Smith, but any baking apple is fine)

### Icing

1/2 cup brown sugar
1/2 cup granulated sugar
1/2 cup cream
1/2 cup butter
1 tablespoon flour
1 teaspoon vanilla

| PER SERVING | |
|---|---|
| CALORIES: | 373 |
| TOTAL FAT: | 20g |
| CHOLESTEROL: | 51mg |
| SODIUM: | 195mg |
| CARBOHYDRATE: | 47g |
| PROTEIN: | 3g |

CAKE: Beat together eggs and oil. Add sugar; mix well. Fold in remaining ingredients. Pour batter into greased and lightly floured 9" x 13" baking dish; bake at 350°F for 50 minutes.

ICING: Boil in a medium saucepan for 2 minutes. Drizzle over each piece of cake just before serving.

# SABBATH DINNER MENU #13

*Contributed by Bonnie Herbel of Caldwell, Idaho*

*Jeanne says:* Bonnie obviously loves people and juggles her roles as a mom and dental assistant with many extracurricular church activities. She loves music and has encouraged both of her children, Katy and Ryan, to take lessons in violin and voice. In addition to all that, Bonnie is an avid walker and clocks in about four miles a day! Her husband Gene has served as farm manager for Gem State Academy for the past twenty years.

*Bonnie says:* As you can see, I like to provide a variety of choices for my Sabbath dinner guests. With all the veggies on the table, anyone who is watching calories can have plenty to eat and still enjoy a low-fat meal. I got the Cabbage Crunch Salad recipe from my good friend Kelly Pflugrad. It is always a big hit whenever I serve it.

**Green-Noodle Casserole**

**Cabbage Crunch Salad**

**Italian Tossed Salad**

**Steamed green beans**

**Corn**

**Sourdough French bread or Italian bread, sliced, buttered, and warmed.**

**Banana Split Dessert**

## Green-Noodle Casserole

serves 10

PER SERVING

CALORIES: 369
TOTAL FAT: 10g
CHOLESTEROL: 19mg
SODIUM: 709mg
CARBOHYDRATE: 49g
PROTEIN: 23g

1 20-ounce can Worthington® *Vegetarian Burger®*
1 tablespoon butter or margarine
2 cups chopped onion
1/8 teaspoon garlic powder
1/4 teaspoon ground oregano
1/2 teaspoon sage
1 teaspoon salt
1 12-ounce package spinach fettuccine, cooked and drained
3 cups low-fat sour cream
3/4 cup grated Parmesan cheese

In a large frying pan, brown onion in butter. Add burger and seasonings. Combine all ingredients in a large bowl. Pour into an oiled 9" x 13" casserole dish. Sprinkle Parmesan cheese over the top. Bake at 350°F for 30 minutes.

## Cabbage Crunch Salad

serves 10

2 tablespoons sesame seeds, toasted
3/4 cup slivered almonds, toasted
1/2 head cabbage, finely chopped
4 green onions, chopped
1 can Worthington® *Fri-Chik®*, chopped
1 package ramen noodles, uncooked and broken

**Dressing**

1/4 teaspoon white pepper
2 tablespoons sugar
1/4 cup white vinegar
1/4 cup lemon juice
3 tablespoons olive oil
3/4 teaspoon salt

PER SERVING

CALORIES: 155
TOTAL FAT: 13g
CHOLESTEROL: 0mg
SODIUM: 271mg
CARBOHYDRATE: 7g
PROTEIN: 5g

Mix all salad ingredients. Add DRESSING just before serving. *The dressing is best if made ahead to let the flavors mix.*

## Italian Tossed Salad

Use a mix of fresh washed and drained lettuces (romaine, red leaf, iceberg, and green leaf)
3 full slices red onion, separate into individual rings
1/2 can whole black olives, drained
2 Roma tomatoes, sliced from top to bottom in 1/2-inch slices
6 to 8 marinated green chilies
Restaurant-style croutons
Italian dressing

## Banana Split Dessert

*serves 12*

1 8-ounce package light cream cheese, softened
1/2 cup sugar
1 20-ounce can crushed pineapple, drained
2 cups partially frozen strawberries, in syrup
2 large firm bananas, chopped
1 12-ounce container light whipped topping
1 cup walnuts, chopped
Whole fresh strawberries, sliced (for garnish)

| PER SERVING | |
| --- | --- |
| CALORIES: | 290 |
| TOTAL FAT: | 13g |
| CHOLESTEROL: | 11mg |
| SODIUM: | 129mg |
| CARBOHYDRATE: | 39g |
| PROTEIN: | 5g |

In a large mixing bowl, beat cream cheese and sugar. Stir in pineapple, frozen strawberries, and bananas. Fold in whipped topping and nuts. Pour into an oiled 9" x 13" x 2" dish. Cover with plastic wrap; freeze until firm, at least 3 hours. Remove from freezer; place in refrigerator 30 minutes before serving. Cut into 3-inch squares. Garnish with a slice of fresh strawberry, leaving the stem on the strawberry.

**Zucchini Bread Pudding**

**Garlic Green Beans**

*Sliced tomatoes and cucumbers*

**Mandarin Orange Cake**

# SABBATH DINNER MENU #14

*Contributed by Del Jean Tabor of Caldwell, Idaho*

*Jeanne says:* "DJ" is a good friend who sings with me in GoodNews, a double mixed quartet. Her calm, thoughtful manner makes her a soothing person to be around. She lives in the country with her husband Calvin and two daughters, Andrea and Kara, and tends a small barnyard of animals including horses, rabbits, and chickens. As if that's not enough to do, she assists her husband in his business as a finish carpenter and works part time as a registered nurse. Her garden keeps her busy (and tanned) in the summer, and it is appropriate that her menu would include lots of fresh veggies, home grown of course!

## Zucchini Bread Pudding

*serves 6*

2 tablespoons olive oil
2 medium zucchini, sliced 1/4-inch thick
1/2 cup frozen whole-kernel corn
1/2 cup chopped roasted red bell pepper (can also use fresh bell pepper)
1 tablespoon minced fresh garlic (6 cloves)
1 tablespoon snipped fresh or 1 teaspoon dried and crushed basil
1 tablespoon snipped fresh or 1 teaspoon dried parsley
1 tablespoon snipped fresh or 1 teaspoon dried and crushed sage
5 cups 1-inch sourdough or Italian bread cubes
1 cup (4 ounces) shredded low-fat Swiss cheese
2 cups low-fat evaporated milk, soymilk, or 2% milk
5 eggs, slightly beaten or 1 1/4 cups Morningstar Farms® *Scramblers*®
1 teaspoon salt

| PER SERVING | |
| --- | --- |
| CALORIES: | 321 |
| TOTAL FAT: | 11g |
| CHOLESTEROL: | 163mg |
| SODIUM: | 834mg |
| CARBOHYDRATE: | 35g |
| PROTEIN: | 20g |

Preheat oven to 350°F. Grease a 2-quart rectangular or oval baking dish; set aside. In a large skillet, cook zucchini and corn in hot oil for 3 minutes. Stir in bell pepper, garlic, basil, parsley, and sage. Cook and stir for 2 minutes more or until zucchini is tender. Stir in bread. Place half the mixture in the prepared dish. Sprinkle with half the cheese. Repeat layers.

In a medium bowl, whisk together milk, eggs, and salt. Carefully pour over bread mixture. Bake uncovered for 35 minutes or until knife inserted near center comes out clean.

*To make ahead:* Layer mixture, but do not bake. Refrigerate for up to 24 hours. Bake uncovered at 350°F for 45 minutes. Let stand for 10 minutes before serving.

## Garlic Green Beans

serves 6

2 pounds fresh green beans
    or 2 14-ounce cans green beans, drained
1 tablespoon butter or margarine
3 tablespoons olive oil

1 medium bulb garlic, peeled and sliced
Salt to taste
1/2 cup grated Parmesan cheese

If using fresh green beans, cook until crisp-tender, about 10 to 15 minutes. Drain; set aside.

Melt butter in a large skillet; stir in olive oil and garlic. Sauté over low heat until garlic is light golden. Stir in green beans and salt; remove from heat. Place in a serving dish; sprinkle with Parmesan cheese.

## Mandarin Orange Cake

serves 15

**Cake**
1 box yellow cake mix
4 eggs
3/4 cup oil
2 8-ounce cans mandarin oranges,
    coarsely chopped (reserve juice
    from 1 can)

**Topping**
1 12-ounce container light
    whipped topping
1 9-ounce can crushed pineapple
    with juice
1 3.4-ounce package instant vanilla
    pudding mix

| PER SERVING | |
| --- | --- |
| CALORIES: | 365 |
| TOTAL FAT: | 19g |
| CHOLESTEROL: | 51mg |
| SODIUM: | 310mg |
| CARBOHYDRATE: | 44g |
| PROTEIN: | 3g |

Beat together cake mix, eggs, and oil. Fold in mandarin oranges and reserved juice. Pour batter into a 9" x 13" baking dish that has been coated with cooking spray. Bake at 350°F for 30 minutes. When cake has cooled, spread with TOPPING.

# Sabbath Dinner Menu #15

*Contributed by Jeanne Jarnes of Caldwell, Idaho*

*Jeanne says:* This Tamale Pie recipe was shared with me by Melinda Blystone, a friend from the Caldwell Church. She brought it to a church potluck, and I fell in love with it. This dish has great flavor and texture (the tofu is frozen first) and is easy to prepare. It contains no cheese or other dairy products, and you'd never guess it was made with tofu!

I adapted the salad recipe from one I found in a magazine, and my mouth starts watering just at the thought of the cilantro/lime dressing! It is unique and absolutely delicious and whips up in minutes. I usually double the recipe so I have dressing to use on salads later in the week.

**Tamale Pie**

**Steamed broccoli and cauliflower florets**

**Black Bean and Avocado Taco Salad**

*Fresh strawberry or peach shortcake*

## Tamale Pie

*serves 8*

1 pound tofu, frozen, thawed, squeezed, and torn into bite-size pieces
2 tablespoons oil
1 medium green bell pepper, chopped
1 medium onion, chopped
2 cloves garlic, minced
2 tablespoons chili powder
1/2 to 1 teaspoon ground cumin
1/2 teaspoon salt

1/4 teaspoon oregano
1 16-ounce can whole tomatoes, chopped
1 15-ounce can tomato sauce
1 10-ounce package frozen corn
1 6-ounce can green chilies, chopped
1/2 cup whole small pitted black olives, drained (can use more)
2 8-ounce packages corn-muffin mix or use the following Cornbread recipe

Sauté pepper, onion, and garlic in oil until transparent. Add tofu pieces, chili powder, cumin, salt, and oregano. Stir and fry for a few minutes, then add tomatoes, tomato sauce, corn, chilies, and olives. Mix well; pour into a 2 1/2-quart casserole dish or a 9" x 13" pan.

Prepare cornbread topping either from corn-muffin mix or Cornbread recipe; spoon evenly over vegetable mixture. Bake at 375°F for about 25 minutes or until cornbread is golden.

| PER SERVING | |
|---|---|
| CALORIES: | 283 |
| TOTAL FAT: | 11g |
| CHOLESTEROL: | 0mg |
| SODIUM: | 874mg |
| CARBOHYDRATE: | 40g |
| PROTEIN: | 10g |

## Cornbread

1 cup cornmeal
1 cup flour
1/4 cup sugar
3 teaspoons baking powder

1 egg
1 cup 2% milk or soymilk
1/4 cup oil
1 teaspoon salt

Combine all ingredients; mix well.

## Black Bean & Avocado Taco Salad

*serves 8*

Cilantro Dressing (recipe follows)
8 cups romaine lettuce, torn into bite-size pieces
2 medium tomatoes, cut into 1/2-inch pieces
2 small cucumbers, unpeeled, diced

1 ripe avocado, diced
3 green onions, sliced
1 15-ounce can black beans, rinsed and drained
2 cups corn chips, slightly crushed

Prepare Cilantro Dressing.

*When ready to serve:* In a large bowl toss all salad ingredients (except corn chips) with dressing. Add corn chips just before placing the salad on the table.

| PER SERVING | |
|---|---|
| CALORIES: | 187 |
| TOTAL FAT: | 9g |
| CHOLESTEROL: | 3mg |
| SODIUM: | 276mg |
| CARBOHYDRATE: | 22g |
| PROTEIN: | 6g |

## Cilantro Dressing

*makes about 1/2 cup*

3 tablespoons fresh lime juice
   (from 2 limes)
1/2 teaspoon lime zest
1/4 cup light mayonnaise
1/2 cup packed fresh cilantro leaves

2 tablespoons light sour cream
1/2 teaspoon ground cumin
1/4 teaspoon sugar
1/8 teaspoon salt

Place lime juice and zest with remaining ingredients in a blender or food processor; blend until smooth, occasionally scraping down sides of blender. *If not using right away, cover and refrigerate.*

**Zucchini Stuffing**

*Salad*

*Corn on the cob*

**Chocolate Zucchini Cake**

*Contributed by Donna and DeAnne Aust of Juneau, Wisconsin*

*Donna and DeAnne say:* We made this casserole dish for Sabbath dinner while Kristi was here in Wisconsin visiting. It is a wonderful dish for the end of summer when everyone seems to have excess zucchini. The original recipe is from our aunt Carol Paulson, who made this years ago when we were visiting in Seattle, Washington. The cake recipe came from a neighbor of ours, a farmer's wife, about twenty years ago. It will make even those who don't like zucchini become instant fans of this versatile squash!

*Kristi says:* It's true! I do not especially dislike zucchini, but you will not find it on my list of favorite foods. When Donna and DeAnne told me they were going to create their menu around a "zucchini theme," I tried to summon a bit of enthusiasm based on the practicality of the idea. I do not remember ever hearing of a zucchini shortage in the summertime. In face, I've often asked my dad why he insists on two zucchini plants in his garden every year; one plant seems to produce enough to keep a small country fed for the month of

August. However, after trying these recipes in Wisconsin, I am looking forward to growing a couple zucchini plants of my own next summer. The cakes and breads are always good, but this casserole—I haven't stopped raving since I tasted it! I should have known that nothing less-than-delicious ever came out the Austs' kitchen.

## Zucchini Stuffing

*serves 8*

5 medium zucchini, cut into $1/2$-inch cubes (fills a 3-quart pan)
6 tablespoons margarine, divided
$3/4$ cup grated carrots
$1/2$ cup chopped onion
2 $1/4$ cups herbed stuffing cubes, divided
1 10.75-ounce can low-fat cream of mushroom soup, undiluted
$1/2$ cup light sour cream

| PER SERVING | |
|---|---|
| CALORIES: | 258 |
| TOTAL FAT: | 11g |
| CHOLESTEROL: | 1mg |
| SODIUM: | 899mg |
| CARBOHYDRATE: | 35g |
| PROTEIN: | 6g |

Cook zucchini in a little boiling, salted water. Drain. Cook carrots and onion in 4 tablespoons margarine. Stir in 1 $1/2$ cups stuffing, soup, and sour cream. Gently stir in zucchini; turn into a 1 $1/2$-quart casserole dish. Melt remaining margarine and toss with remaining cubes; top casserole. Bake at 350°F for 30 to 40 minutes.

## Chocolate Zucchini Cake

*serves 15*

1/2 cup soft butter
1/2 cup oil
1 3/4 cups sugar
2 eggs
1 teaspoon vanilla
1/2 cup 2% milk
1 teaspoon lemon juice
2 1/2 cups flour
1/4 teaspoon salt
4 tablespoons cocoa

1 teaspoon baking soda
1/2 teaspoon cinnamon
1/2 teaspoon cloves
2 cups grated zucchini, drained

**Topping**
1/2 cup chopped nuts
1/2 cup chocolate chips
3 tablespoons sugar

| PER SERVING | |
|---|---|
| CALORIES: | 378 |
| TOTAL FAT: | 19g |
| CHOLESTEROL: | 42mg |
| SODIUM: | 196mg |
| CARBOHYDRATE: | 49g |
| PROTEIN: | 5g |

Cream butter, oil, and sugar. Combine eggs, vanilla, milk, and lemon juice. Mix alternately with dry ingredients. Fold in zucchini. Pour into a greased and floured 9" x 13" pan. Top with nuts, chocolate chips, and sugar. Bake at 350°F for 50 minutes.

# SABBATH DINNER MENU #17

*Contributed by Kristen Jarnes of Spokane, Washington*

*Kristi says:* This menu has grown and changed through the past few years as I've found new recipes to include and adapted some of the older ones. I first made this casserole in college, and it soon became my throw-it-together-at-the-last-minute Friday afternoon standby when I was too exhausted to do anything except boil some water and open a can. I have since added the sautéed burger and sometimes even mix a package of thawed frozen spinach into the casserole.

The salad is just one of the delicious recipes that I brought back from Ukraine. My friends there often cooked with eggplant, although they rarely served it the same way twice (and never in the form of eggplant parmesan)! By the time I left Kiev, the *baklazhanya* dishes had become some of my favorite.

This cake has also become a favorite since I first came across it while living in Michigan a few years ago. It is easy to make, but doesn't look or taste like it. The different layers make a striking presentation when the pieces are cut and served. It's a truly irresistible dessert—no wonder they call it Italian Love Cake!

**Baked Mostaccioli**

*Baklazhanya (Eggplant) Salad*

*Broccoli*

*Fresh garlic bread*

Italian Love Cake

## Baked Mostaccioli

*serves 12*

1 16-ounce package mostaccioli pasta, uncooked
3 tablespoons olive oil
1 medium onion, chopped
1 large green pepper, chopped
1 20-ounce can Worthington® *Low-Fat Vegetarian Burger®*
1 teaspoon salt
1 teaspoon dried basil
1 teaspoon dried oregano
1 tablespoon dried parsley
2 or 3 cloves garlic, minced or pressed
1 6-ounce can tomato paste
1 28-ounce can Italian-seasoned stewed tomatoes (reserve liquid)
1 8-ounce package low-fat mozzarella cheese, shredded

| PER SERVING | |
|---|---|
| CALORIES: | 319 |
| TOTAL FAT: | 10g |
| CHOLESTEROL: | 17mg |
| SODIUM: | 742mg |
| CARBOHYDRATE: | 39g |
| PROTEIN: | 18g |

Cook pasta as directed on package. In the meantime, sauté onion and pepper in olive oil until tender. Add burger and seasonings; fry until lightly browned. Stir in garlic, tomato paste, and reserved liquid from stewed tomatoes. Combine burger and mostaccioli noodles; spread evenly in a 9" x 13" casserole. Cover with stewed tomatoes; top with mozzarella cheese. Bake covered at 350°F for 30 minutes. Remove foil; bake for another 5 minutes or until cheese is lightly browned.

## Baklazhanya (Eggplant) Salad

*serves 8*

1 small eggplant, peeled and cubed
1/3 cup light sour cream
1 tablespoon lemon juice
1 tablespoon chopped parsley
1 teaspoon salt
1 teaspoon dill weed
1 clove garlic, minced
2 teaspoons melted butter or olive oil
1 cup restaurant-style croutons
1 head red leaf or romaine lettuce, torn into bite-size pieces

| PER SERVING | |
| --- | --- |
| CALORIES: | 54 |
| TOTAL FAT: | 2g |
| CHOLESTEROL: | 1mg |
| SODIUM: | 334mg |
| CARBOHYDRATE: | 8g |
| PROTEIN: | 1g |

Cook eggplant, covered, in 1 inch of boiling salted water for about 5 minutes or until just tender. Drain; refrigerate for at least 30 minutes.

In a separate bowl, mix sour cream, lemon juice, parsley, salt, dill, and garlic. Cover; chill in the refrigerator.

*When ready to serve:* Toss croutons in butter or oil; combine with lettuce, eggplant, and sour cream mixture. *For variety you can also add chopped tomatoes, olives, artichoke hearts, and/or crumbled feta cheese.*

## Italian Love Cake

*serves 15*

**Cake**
1 box chocolate cake mix
2 pounds low-fat Ricotta cheese
3/4 cup sugar
1 teaspoon vanilla
4 eggs

**Raspberry Layer**
1 12-ounce package
    frozen raspberries, thawed

1/4 cup cold water
1 tablespoon cornstarch
1/4 cup sugar

**Frosting**
1 6-ounce box instant chocolate
    pudding
1 cup 2% or skim milk
1 8-ounce container light whipped
    topping

| PER SERVING | |
|---|---|
| CALORIES: | 320 |
| TOTAL FAT: | 11g |
| CHOLESTEROL: | 75mg |
| SODIUM: | 668mg |
| CARBOHYDRATE: | 45g |
| PROTEIN: | 13g |

Mix CAKE according to directions on box; pour into a greased and floured 9" x 13" baking dish. Combine remaining CAKE ingredients; pour evenly over top of unbaked cake. Bake at 350°F for 60 to 70 minutes. Let cool; invert cake onto platter or aluminum-foil-covered cookie sheet.

RASPBERRY LAYER: Heat raspberries just to boiling in small saucepan. Meanwhile, stir cornstarch into cold water until dissolved; add to berries. Heat until mixture boils again; turn heat down. Add sugar; stir until thickened to glazelike consistency. Spread over cool cake. Place in the refrigerator or freezer for a few minutes until set.

FROSTING: Mix pudding with milk; fold in whipped topping. Spread on sides and top of cake; refrigerate. Serve cake on dessert plates drizzled with chocolate or raspberry syrup.

*Note: Raspberry syrup can be made by thinning 1/4 cup seedless raspberry jam with water.*

# SABBATH DINNER MENU # 18

*Contributed by Deborah Grove of Niles, Michigan*

*Kristi says:* Debbie and I became friends our freshman year at Takoma Academy. She was not an Adventist when she began attending TA, and we soon began calling our lunch periods in the cafeteria "veggie adventures" as she bravely tried out *Big Franks®, Choplets®, FriChik®,* and that mysterious *Nuteena®* in front of her highly amused friends. However, her absolute favorite food discovery—much to my surprise—was the haystacks. I had grown up eating them at church potlucks and picnics, but Debbie raved about "the perfect meal" so much that I developed a new appreciation for haystacks and found myself looking forward to Wednesdays in the cafeteria almost as much as she did. Who would have guessed?

Now Debbie is a pastor's wife and cooking up veggie adventures of her own, like this spinach meatball recipe, which came from a church member in Lansdale, Pennsylvania. When their Pathfinder group decided to sell these meatballs in hoagie sandwiches at the Pathfinder Fair a few years ago, they were so popular that the chefs couldn't keep up with the demand. I specifically asked her to include them in her menu.

**"Pathfinder" Spinach Balls**

**Cabbage Salad**

**Chinese Noodle Drops**

## "Pathfinder" Spinach Balls

*makes 30 balls*

| PER SERVING | |
|---|---|
| CALORIES: | 97 |
| TOTAL FAT: | 5g |
| CHOLESTEROL: | 39mg |
| SODIUM: | 313mg |
| CARBOHYDRATE: | 101g |
| PROTEIN: | 4g |

1 10-ounce package frozen spinach
6 eggs or 1 1/2 cups Morningstar Farms® *Scramblers*®
1 cup Parmesan cheese
1 8-ounce bag herb stuffing
1/4 to 1/2 cup butter or margarine, melted
1 onion, chopped
1 26-ounce jar prepared spaghetti sauce

Cook frozen spinach; drain well. Mix with eggs, cheese, stuffing, margarine, and onion. Let sit for 5 minutes until liquid is absorbed. Form into 1 1/2-inch balls; bake at 350°F for 15 to 20 minutes, or until golden brown. Add to hot spaghetti sauce; serve over pasta or in a hoagie roll.

## Cabbage Salad

*serves 10*

1 package Ramen noodles
1/2 head red or green cabbage, chopped
3 green onions
1/4 cup sunflower seeds, toasted
1/2 cup sliced almonds, toasted

**Dressing**
1/2 cup oil
2 teaspoons sugar
1 teaspoon chickenlike seasoning and broth mix

| PER SERVING | |
|---|---|
| CALORIES: | 166 |
| TOTAL FAT: | 17g |
| CHOLESTEROL: | 0mg |
| SODIUM: | 67mg |
| CARBOHYDRATE: | 4g |
| PROTEIN: | 2g |

Mix all salad ingredients together; add DRESSING. *If possible, chill salad for an hour or two before serving. (If you want the noodles to be crunchy, wait to put them in until just before serving.)*

## Chinese Noodle Drops

*makes about 46*

1 12-ounce bag peanut-butter chips
1 12-ounce bag chocolate chips
1 8.5-ounce can chowmein noodles, broken

| PER SERVING | |
|---|---|
| CALORIES: | 98 |
| TOTAL FAT: | 6g |
| CHOLESTEROL: | 1mg |
| SODIUM: | 38mg |
| CARBOHYDRATE: | 10g |
| PROTEIN: | 2g |

Melt chips. Add noodles. Drop teaspoon-size "candies" onto wax paper. Let cool.

**Chicken Wrap-Ups**

**Summer Squash Casserole**

*Tossed salad*

**German Sweet Chocolate Brownies**

# SABBATH DINNER MENU #19

*Contributed by Meghan Titcomb of Columbus, Ohio*

*Kristi says:* Meghan and I met and became good friends in college. We used to exercise together often and probably covered hundreds of miles of Michigan roads over the years. We also spent a very, very long summer working as servers at the same restaurant. It was so nice to have someone who understood the frustration and exhaustion of trying to please customers and managers all day—and the moments of flying high when it seemed like you were actually succeeding. I have always appreciated Meghan's ability to keep her life in balance both spiritually and healthfully.

*Meghan says:* I usually don't have tons of side dishes, since I'm cooking just for me. I like to have salad, some other kind of vegetable, and some bread or rolls, the way my mom served these recipes when I was growing up. Busy families don't have time for anythig elaborate. Also, these entrees are so filling and nutritious that you don't need much more for a balanced meal. These recipes are, for the most part, quick and easy; to me that's important when you have a busy schedule!

## Chicken Wrap-Ups

*serves 8*

| PER SERVING | |
|---|---|
| CALORIES: | 230 |
| TOTAL FAT: | 16g |
| CHOLESTEROL: | 23mg |
| SODIUM: | 451mg |
| CARBOHYDRATE: | 12g |
| PROTEIN: | 7g |

6 ounces light cream cheese
2 tablespoons margarine
1/8 teaspoon garlic powder
1/8 teaspoon oregano
2 tablespoons reserved *Diced Chik®* gravy

1 tablespoon chopped pimento (optional)
1 can Worthington® *Diced Chik®* (reserve gravy)
1 tube ready-to-bake refrigerated crescent rolls

In a large bowl, combine cream cheese, margarine, garlic powder, oregano, reserved gravy, and pimento. Add *Diced Chik®;* mix well. Split open the tube of crescent rolls; separate squares but not triangles. Press together diagonal perforation in each square; fill with 3 tablespoons filling. Fold one corner of the dough to meet the opposite corner in the center. Do the same with the other 2 corners; pinch edges to seal. Bake at 350° F for 15 to 20 minutes until golden brown.

## Summer Squash Casserole

*serves 10*

| PER SERVING | |
|---|---|
| CALORIES: | 56 |
| TOTAL FAT: | 3g |
| CHOLESTEROL: | 10mg |
| SODIUM: | 52mg |
| CARBOHYDRATE: | 5g |
| PROTEIN: | 3g |

3 medium yellow summer squash, sliced
1 large onion, sliced
1 14.5-ounce can Italian stewed tomatoes, undrained
1 cup shredded mozzarella cheese

Steam summer squash and onion until tender. In a 2-quart casserole dish, layer half of the summer squash and onions, half of the tomatoes, and half of the cheese. Repeat layers. Bake at 350°F for 20 minutes or until bubbly and cheese begins to brown.

## German Sweet Chocolate Brownies

*serves 16*

1 4-ounce package sweet baking chocolate
1/4 cup butter or margarine
3/4 cup brown sugar, divided
2 eggs
1/2 cup flour
1 cup chopped pecans or walnuts, divided
1 1/3 cups grated coconut
1/4 cup 2% milk

| PER SERVING | |
| --- | --- |
| CALORIES: | 189 |
| TOTAL FAT: | 14g |
| CHOLESTEROL: | 24mg |
| SODIUM: | 62mg |
| CARBOHYDRATE: | 16g |
| PROTEIN: | 4g |

Microwave chocolate and butter on high for 1 1/2 minutes; stir until chocolate is melted. Stir 1/2 cup brown sugar into chocolate/butter mixture until well blended. Mix in eggs. Stir in flour and 1/2 cup nuts until blended. Spread into an 8" x 8" pan. Mix coconut, 1/4 cup brown sugar, and 1/2 cup nuts in a bowl; stir in milk until well blended. Spoon evenly over brownie batter. Bake at 350°F for 35 minutes (325°F if you're using a glass pan). Check periodically; brownies are done when a toothpick comes out clean without crumbs.

# SABBATH DINNER MENU #20

*Contributed by Gayle Beck of College Place, Washington*

*Jeanne says:* One of the things my sister-in-law Gayle and I have in common is that we love to try new recipes. She gave me a subscription to *Vegetarian Times* magazine for Christmas last year, and we are always comparing notes about new yummy recipes we've discovered.

*Gayle says:* The cashew Chic-kett casserole is a recipe I have adapted for vegetarians. This quick-and-easy recipe is a little bit spicy—but not too much. Years ago a friend shared the Peach Kuchen recipe with me. It is not an authentic German kuchen, but it is yummie just the same and fast to prepare.

**Cashew Chic-ketts**

**Whole fresh green beans, steamed**

**Tossed green salad**

**Whole-wheat rolls**

**Peach Kuchen**

## Cashew Chic-ketts

*serves 6*

1 16-ounce roll Worthington® *Chic-ketts*®*
1/4 teaspoon salt
1 large clove garlic, minced or pressed
1 egg white
2 tablespoons cornstarch
2 tablespoons peanut or corn oil
1 1/2 tablespoons vegetable oil
1 red bell pepper, cut into 1/2-inch squares

1 green bell pepper, cut into 1/2-inch squares
1 cup sliced scallions (about 1 bunch—substitute
   green onions if scallions aren't available)
1 8-ounce can sliced water chestnuts, drained
2 tablespoons (vegetarian) Hoisin sauce
1/2 cup chickenlike seasoning and broth mix
1 or 2 teaspoons chili paste (with garlic)
3/4 cup roasted cashews

Cut or tear partially thawed *Chic-ketts*® into 1/2-inch cubes. In a medium bowl, combine chicken with salt, garlic, egg white, and cornstarch. Toss to coat evenly. In a wok or a 10-inch skillet, heat peanut or cornoil over high heat until very hot. Add *Chic-ketts*®; stir-fry for 3 to 4 minutes. Remove to a plate.

Heat vegetable oil in the wok. Add peppers, scallions, and water chestnuts. Stir-fry until crisp-tender, about 2 minutes. Remove to a plate with *Chic-ketts*®.

Put Hoisin sauce, broth, and chili paste in the wok; simmer over low heat for 2 minutes. Increase heat to high; return *Chic-ketts*® and vegetables to the wok. Stir-fry 1 to 2 minutes or until heated through. Stir in cashews.

*\* This entree can also be made with firm tofu. To remove excess water: Slice the tofu block into three sections, then place on a plate covered with several layers of paper towels. Place another plate on top; put a heavy object on it to press water out.*

| PER SERVING | |
| --- | --- |
| CALORIES: | 291 |
| TOTAL FAT: | 18g |
| CHOLESTEROL: | >1mg |
| SODIUM: | 951mg |
| CARBOHYDRATE: | 13g |
| PROTEIN: | 19g |

## Peach Kuchen

*serves 15*

1 box white cake mix
1/2 cup flaked coconut, toasted
1 cube butter or margarine
3 cups sliced fresh or canned peaches
2 tablespoons sugar
1/2 teaspoon cinnamon
1 cup light sour cream
1 egg

| PER SERVING | |
| --- | --- |
| CALORIES: | 222 |
| TOTAL FAT: | 12g |
| CHOLESTEROL: | 30mg |
| SODIUM: | 247mg |
| CARBOHYDRATE: | 28g |
| PROTEIN: | 2g |

Combine cake mix and coconut. Cut in butter until mixture resembles coarse crumbs. Lightly press into bottom and 1/2 inch up sides of a 13" x 9" x 2" baking dish.

*Friday preparation:* Bake crust at 350°F for 15 to 20 minutes; allow to cool. Cover.

*On Sabbath:* Before dinner, arrange peaches over crust. Combine sugar and cinnamon; sprinkle evenly over peaches. Blend sour cream and egg; pour over all. *I like to drizzle the mixture back and forth to make a design.* Bake again for 10 to 15 minutes while preparing dinner, until sour-cream mixture is set. Let cool while eating dinner. Serve warm.

**Enchiladas**

**Whole-kernel corn**

**Green salad**

# SABBATH DINNER MENU #21

*Contributed by Helen Stiles of Boise, Idaho*

*Jeanne says:* Helen is editorial secretary for the *Signs of the Times* team at Pacific Press and works closely with my husband, Dave. She highly recommends these enchiladas as the best she's ever made!

## Enchiladas

*makes 10*

| PER SERVING | |
|---|---|
| CALORIES: | 199 |
| TOTAL FAT: | 11g |
| CHOLESTEROL: | 20mg |
| SODIUM: | 232mg |
| CARBOHYDRATE: | 20g |
| PROTEIN: | 6g |

1 12.5-ounce can Worthington® *FriChik*®,
   sliced as for chicken strips (reserve gravy)
1/2 large onion, chopped
1 cup cooked rice
1 cup grated cheddar cheese, divided
Salt to taste
10 corn tortillas
Vegetable oil
1 15-ounce can mild enchilada sauce

*Filling:* Fry *Fri-Chik*® with onion. Add rice; continue to fry until well flavored. When done, add 1/2 cup cheese and salt.

In a bowl, mix enchilada sauce and reserved *FriChik*® gravy. In the bottom of a medium-size glass baking dish or pan (not the huge potluck size), place about 1/2 cup enchilada sauce mixture. Warm tortillas 4 at a time (see instructions below). Fill and roll enchiladas, placing them in the pan seam side down. Cover with remaining sauce. Bake at 350°F for 35 minutes or until bubbly, covering lightly with foil for the last 15 minutes. Take out and sprinkle with remaining 1/2 cup cheese; bake for another 10 minutes—just to melt cheese.

*Tortilla preparation:* To make the corn tortillas soft enough to roll, place a little oil on your hands. Wipe each tortilla top and bottom with oiled hands, placing 4 at a time on a plate, fan shape (not stacked). Microwave for 1 minute while you prepare the next 4. *These will be soft enough to roll and not break.* Sprinkle each tortilla with a little salt before rolling.

**Sabbath Soup Buffet**

**Apple-Bleu Cheese Salad With Caramelized Pecans**

*Garlic bread or bread sticks*

*Cranberry drink or hot herb tea (depending on the season)*

*Fresh Coconut Cream Pie*

# SABBATH DINNER MENU #22

*Contributed by LaJean Botimer of Nampa, Idaho*

*Jeanne says:* Here is an unusual idea for a Sabbath buffet, offered by a very classy lady and superb cook. LaJean enjoys cooking, reading, golf, and most of all, her four grandchildren: Mindy, Krysten, Allen, and Jeffrey—all of them wonderful musicians who play the harp, piano, flute, violin, and guitar and love to sing! She and her husband are active leaders in their local church and supporters of Gem State Academy activities. It's not uncommon to find them running a cookie table as a fundraiser during a Saturday-night basketball game—homemade cookies, of course! Every community deserves to have active retirees like these!

*Jackie says:* LaJean and I used to share carpooling duties when our children attended Seattle Junior Academy. What a small world!

*LaJean says:* I use the stove and kitchen counters to create a buffet. Provide the guests with large soup bowls, and they can add to their soup whatever makes them happy. This makes it easy for dieters, children, or fussy eaters to have just what they like. And it can expand to however many guests you happen to invite home for dinner! For dessert, you can make the Fresh Coconut Cream Pie from scratch with tons of calories or use coconut pudding mix with low-fat milk and add fresh coconut.

## Sabbath Soup Buffet

1 crockpot with chickenlike seasoning and broth mix
1 crockpot with cream soup base (make your favorite thin white sauce*)
Sautéed carrots, celery, onions
Cooked diced potatoes or mashed potatoes, heated
Corn kernels, heated
Beans, heated (your choice: kidney, black, pinto, etc.)
Broccoli florets, cooked
Chopped meat substitute of your choice
Grated cheddar cheese

*Note: You may wish to use the Basic Vegan Cream Sauce (p. 78).*

## Apple-Bleu Cheese Salad W/ Caramelized Pecans

*serves 10*

4 Granny Smith apples, sliced
1 cup crumbled blue cheese
1 head leaf or bibb lettuce

1 head romaine lettuce
1 cup red cabbage
1 cup Caramelized Pecans (recipe follows)

Toss salad with Orange or Lemon Vinaigrette Dressing (recipes follow).

## Caramelized Pecans

1 cup brown sugar
2 cups raw pecans
4 tablespoons water

Mix together brown sugar and pecans. Place flat on cookie sheet; bake at 350°F for 10 minutes. Stir in water; mix. Bake an additional 10 minutes, stirring repeatedly until water has evaporated (approximately 40 minutes). Scrape with a spatula before completely cooled.

## Orange Vinaigrette

1 cup frozen orange juice concentrate
1/2 cup apple cider vinegar or lemon juice
1/4 cup canola oil
2 packets sugar substitute

| PER SERVING (ORANGE VINAIGRETTE) | |
| --- | --- |
| CALORIES: | 291 |
| TOTAL FAT: | 17g |
| CHOLESTEROL: | 10mg |
| SODIUM: | 206mg |
| CARBOHYDRATE: | 32g |
| PROTEIN: | 7g |

## Lemon Vinaigrette

1/2 white onion
2 cloves garlic
Juice of 2 lemons
1/2 cup apple cider vinegar

1 1/2 cups salad oil
1/8 cup sugar
Salt, white pepper, and Tabasco®
   to taste

## Fresh Coconut Cream Pie

*serves 8*

2/3 cup sugar
3 1/2 tablespoons cornstarch
1/2 teaspoon salt
1/2 cup cold 2% milk
2 cups half-and-half
3 egg yolks
1 teaspoon vanilla

1 tablespoon butter
1/3 cup fresh coconut (in small
   chunks)
2/3 cup sweetened shredded
   coconut, divided
1 9-inch baked pie shell

| PER SERVING | |
| --- | --- |
| CALORIES: | 236 |
| TOTAL FAT: | 14g |
| CHOLESTEROL: | 107mg |
| SODIUM: | 185mg |
| CARBOHYDRATE: | 25g |
| PROTEIN: | 4g |

Combine sugar, cornstarch, and salt in the top of a double boiler. Stir in milk and half-and-half. Cook over boiling water until thickened, stirring constantly. Cover; cook 15 minutes longer. Stir a little of the hot mixture into slightly beaten egg yolks; add to remaining mixture in the double boiler. Cook for 2 minutes over hot (not boiling) water, stirring constantly. Add butter; cool. Add vanilla. Sprinkle 1/3 cup shredded coconut in bottom of pie shell. Add remaining coconut to filling. Spoon into pie shell. Chill; top with a small amount of whipped cream.

**Chickpea Stew**

*Cucumber salad*

**Whole-wheat bread with
peanut butter**

**Macaroon Pineapple Whip**

*Contributed by Barbara Wareham of Loma Linda, California*

*Jackie says:* Barbara and I have known each other since junior camp and academy days in Keene, Texas. She and her husband, Dr. Ellsworth E. Wareham, have been associated with Loma Linda University for all of their professional lives. Dr. Wareham, a cardiac surgeon, founded the overseas heart-surgery program, along with Dr. Joan Coggin. Since 1963, the heart-surgery team has performed heart surgeries and established cardiac-surgery programs throughout the world. Barbara accompanied her husband whenever she could. They have five children and eight grandchildren.

*Barbara says:* Wherever we went, we were invited to people's homes for Sabbath dinner. I always think of the time we spent in Athens, Greece. We had been in Suchou, China, in the early days after China was opened to the U.S. Food was scarce, and we were all still hungry after each meal. We left China and flew to Athens, Greece, where we went home with the pastor, Nick

Germanis. For Sabbath dinner his wife fixed a huge tureen of this chickpea stew, a cucumber salad, and thick slices of whole-wheat bread with peanut butter. To this day it's the most memorable meal I've ever experienced!

## Chickpea Stew

*serves 6*

3/4 cup dried chickpeas (garbanzo beans)
　　or 1 15-ounce can garbanzo beans
5 cups vegetable stock
1 pound baking potatoes, peeled and diced
1 pound tomatoes, peeled and chopped (optional)

2 teaspoons *garam masala* (curry powder)
1/2 teaspoon ground ginger
1/2 teaspoon ground turmeric
Salt to taste
3 tablespoons chopped fresh cilantro

| PER SERVING | |
| --- | --- |
| CALORIES: | 183 |
| TOTAL FAT: | 6g |
| CHOLESTEROL: | 0mg |
| SODIUM: | 19mg |
| CARBOHYDRATE: | 29g |
| PROTEIN: | 6g |

If using dried chickpeas, place in a bowl; add water to cover generously. Soak for 3 hours; drain.

In a saucepan over high heat, bring vegetable stock to a boil. Add chickpeas, reduce heat to medium. Simmer, uncovered, until almost tender (about 1 1/2 hours). Add potatoes, tomatoes, *masala,* ginger, and turmeric; continue to cook until chickpeas are tender (about 30 minutes longer). Remove from heat; let cool slightly. Transfer half of the stock and vegetables to a blender or food processor; purée until smooth. Return to saucepan; season with salt to taste. Reheat to serving temperature. Ladle into warm bowls, sprinkle with cilantro; serve hot.

## Macaroon Pineapple Whip

*serves 8*

*Barbara says:* Here is a quickie dessert I make when I bring company home from church unexpectedly. A local bakery sells big, fat, soft macaroons. I try to keep a dozen in my freezer for future use, as well as whipped topping, and a can or two of pineapple chunks in my pantry.

| PER SERVING | |
| --- | --- |
| CALORIES: | 284 |
| TOTAL FAT: | 12g |
| CHOLESTEROL: | 0mg |
| SODIUM: | 96mg |
| CARBOHYDRATE: | 41g |
| PROTEIN: | 2g |

8 to 10 large, soft coconut macaroons
1 20-ounce can pineapple chunks, chilled
1 8-ounce container light whipped topping
1/2 to 1 cup broken pecans

Break up or coarsely crumble macaroons (not too fine). Pour pineapple juice over the macaroons; let soak during lunch. *Drain off any juice so they won't be watery.* Fold in pineapple chunks, pecans, and whipped topping. *The longer it sits, the better the flavor.* Serve in dessert dishes.

# SABBATH DINNER MENU #24

*Contributed by Barbara Wareham of Loma Linda, California*

*Barbara says:* The vegan recipe for cream sauce used in this stroganoff can be adapted to make several different dishes. For example, I add soya cheese to make a delicious cheese sauce; basil and cayenne to make alfredo sauce; and soy sauce, chicken seasoning, or Vegex® to make a gravy. It can be used for everything from scalloped potatoes to casseroles and contains no dairy products!

I always like to serve something sweet with a rice dish. The ambrosia salad is a perfect complement to the stroganoff and rice. Be sure to toss the spinach salad often while at the table as all the good stuff tends to fall to the bottom! Although the Canadian Mud Pie recipe sounds difficult to make, it isn't—and it is delicious.

**Vegan Stroganoff**

**Molded Ambrosia Salad**

**Spinach Salad**

**Asparagus**

**Canadian Mud Pie (Vegan)**

## Vegan Stroganoff

*serves 8*

1 cup diced onion
1 cup diced celery
1 cup diced green or red bell pepper (optional)

Vegan Cream Sauce (recipe follows)
1 20-ounce can Worthington® Choplets®
   cut into $1/2$-inch strips

Sauté vegetables; set aside. Prepare Vegan Cream Sauce; pour into sautéed vegetables. Bring to a boil, stirring constantly. Add *Choplets*®; cook until hot. Serve over brown rice or pasta.

## Basic Vegan Cream Sauce

1 cup raw cashews or blanched almonds
3 cups water
2 tablespoons unbleached white flour
1 teaspoon salt
1 tablespoon chickenlike seasoning and broth mix
$1/2$ teaspoon onion powder
$1/2$ teaspoon celery salt

| PER SERVING | |
| --- | --- |
| CALORIES: | 167 |
| TOTAL FAT: | 9g |
| CHOLESTEROL: | 0mg |
| SODIUM: | 875mg |
| CARBOHYDRATE: | 12g |
| PROTEIN: | 12g |

Place cashews or almonds into blender. Add one cup of water and blend until very, very smooth and creamy. Add flour, salt, chicken seasoning, onion powder, and celery salt; continue blending. In a saucepan, bring 2 cups of water to a boil. Add blended mixture to boiling water and stir constantly while bringing to a second boil. Remove from heat.

## Molded Ambrosia Salad

*serves 8*

1 3-ounce package orange gelatin
1 cup boiling water
1 cup undrained crushed pineapple
1 4-ounce can mandarin oranges, drained
1/2 cup chopped pecans
1/2 cup nondairy sour cream substitute
1/2 cup light whipped topping
1/3 cup sugar

| PER SERVING | |
|---|---|
| CALORIES: | 186 |
| TOTAL FAT: | 8g |
| CHOLESTEROL: | 0mg |
| SODIUM: | 49mg |
| CARBOHYDRATE: | 27g |
| PROTEIN: | 2g |

Dissolve gelatin with boiling water; add undrained pineapple. Cool slightly until beginning to set. Add oranges and pecans. Combine sour cream substitute, whipped topping, and sugar; add to gelatin mixture. Pour into a 6-cup mold; chill until firm.

## Spinach Salad

*serves 10*

2 bunches fresh spinach, cut into 1-inch strips
1 cauliflower, blended into the size of peas (Be careful not to blend too much!)
1 to 2 cups sliced fresh mushrooms
2 to 3 avocados, sliced
1/2 cup dried cranberries (optional)
1/2 cup mandarin orange segments or slices of mango
Chopped walnuts to taste
Favorite vinaigrette (with a dash nutmeg added)
Walnut halves (for garnish)

| PER SERVING | |
|---|---|
| CALORIES: | 96 |
| TOTAL FAT: | 8g |
| CHOLESTEROL: | 0mg |
| SODIUM: | 12mg |
| CARBOHYDRATE: | 6g |
| PROTEIN: | 2g |

Place spinach, cauliflower, mushrooms, avocados, optional fruit, and chopped walnuts on a shallow platter. Drizzle with dressing; toss very gently. Garnish with walnut halves.

## Asparagus

Sauté asparagus in a small amount of olive or sesame oil, sprinkle with juice from half a lemon. When asparagus is "crisp done," toss with toasted pine nuts or sesame seeds.

## Canadian Mud Pie (Vegan)

*serves 8*

Pear Ice Cream (recipe follows)
Crumb Crust (recipe follows)
1/2 cup carob chips
1 to 2 tablespoons coffee substitute
1 8-ounce container light whipped topping

Prepare Pear Ice Cream as directed.

Prepare Crumb Crust, let cool. When Pear Ice Cream is frozen, remove from freezer; cut into small cubes. Purée cubes in a food processor or blender. *(Add a little tofu milk to help make it smooth.)* Pour into crust; return to freezer.

Remove from freezer 20 to 30 minutes before serving; thaw until it can be sliced. *Pie should still be quite firm.* In a double boiler, melt carob chips and coffee substitute. *(Be careful, carob melts very quickly! I've found it is much better to melt it over hot water than in the microwave.)* Garnish each piece of pie with a drizzle of melted carob mixture and a big dollop of nondairy whipped topping.

| PER SERVING | |
|---|---|
| CALORIES: | 439 |
| TOTAL FAT: | 22g |
| CHOLESTEROL: | 0mg |
| SODIUM: | 143mg |
| CARBOHYDRATE: | 60g |
| PROTEIN: | 5g |

## Canadian Mud Pie (continued)

## Pear Ice Cream

*serves 8*

1 cup raw cashews
1 cup pear juice (from canned pears)
1/4 teaspoon salt
1 teaspoon vanilla
1/3 cup honey or maple syrup
1/4 cup tofu milk
1 quart or 2 15-ounce cans pears, drained

Place cashews and pear juice in blender; blend until creamy. *Do not underblend.* Add remaining ingredients; blend well again. Pour mixture into a flat 9" x 12" container; cover and freeze.

## Crumb Crust

*makes 1
8-inch
pie crust*

1 cup graham cracker crumbs
1/2 cup unbleached white flour
1/3 cup maple syrup
3 tablespoons vegetable oil or 1/2 cup cashews or pecans, finely ground

Preheat oven to 350°F. Mix graham cracker crumbs and flour together in a small bowl. Slowly cut maple syrup and oil or nuts into the dry ingredients until the mixture just holds together when compressed. Pat crumb mixture evenly over the bottom of a lightly oiled 8-inch pie plate or 8" x 8" pan. Bake for 10 minutes or until golden brown. Cool.

**Baptist Dish**

*Cranberry sauce*

**Baked Asparagus**

**Scalloped Potatoes**

**Layered Salad**

**Raspberry Cream Pie**

*Contributed by Betty Jo King of Oshawa, Ontario, Canada*

*Jackie says:* When we lived in Oshawa, Betty Jo was "the hostess with the mostess"! She seemed to invite people to their home nearly every Sabbath, and she prepared such delicious meals. It was a special privilege to be her guest. When my husband, Ed, was in a near-fatal car accident in Sault Ste. Marie, Ontario, Betty Jo's husband, Dr. Archie King, provided excellent care as the supervising physician who coordinated the nine surgeries Ed needed in the seven months that followed. Even though Dr. Archie has now passed away, he and Betty Jo will always be very special people to Ed and me.

*Betty Jo says:* This menu is a King family favorite for Sabbath dinner. We call the entree the "Baptist Dish" in memory of one of Archie's Baptist patients, who gave us the recipe. The original recipe called for beef, but I adapted it to use *Choplets*®. I have always tried to cook for Sabbath on Friday; with 3 children of my own, plus 5 adopted children, a good schedule was a must. So, Thursday was for house cleaning, Friday was for cooking, and Sabbath was for enjoying family and friends!

## Baptist Dish

serves 8

| PER SERVING | |
|---|---|
| CALORIES: | 270 |
| TOTAL FAT: | 19g |
| CHOLESTEROL: | 54mg |
| SODIUM: | 471mg |
| CARBOHYDRATE: | 12g |
| PROTEIN: | 14g |

1 20-ounce can Worthington® *Low-Fat Choplets®*, diced (reserve liquid)
1 teaspoon Marmite® or Vegex®, dissolved in 1 cup hot water
2 eggs or 1/2 cup Morningstar Farms® *Scramblers®*
1/2 cup light mayonnaise
1 cup 2% milk
4 tablespoons soft butter or margarine
4 tablespoons flour
1/2 cup slivered almonds
1 cup Chinese noodles

*Betty Jo says:* I dice the entire can of *Choplets®* and then use the liquid from the *Choplets®* toward my 1 cup hot water. Beat the eggs slightly. Then combine all ingredients. *Couldn't be easier!* Place in a greased 2-quart casserole. Put the casserole in a baking pan that has been filled with water. Bake at 350°F for 60 minutes.

## Baked Asparagus

serves 8

Spray a cookie sheet with olive oil. Put one layer of asparagus spears on the cookie sheet; sprinkle with coarse salt. Brush the tops of the spears with olive oil. Bake at 325°F for 10 minutes. *M-m-m!!*

## Scalloped Potatoes

*serves 8*

6 to 8 potatoes
1 tablespoon butter
4 tablespoons flour
2 cups 2% milk

Salt to taste
1/2 cup sliced onions
1/2 cup grated cheese

| PER SERVING | |
| --- | --- |
| CALORIES: | 185 |
| TOTAL FAT: | 5g |
| CHOLESTEROL: | 12mg |
| SODIUM: | 365mg |
| CARBOHYDRATE: | 29g |
| PROTEIN: | 7g |

*On Friday:* Parboil potatoes; peel and slice. Melt butter; remove from heat. Stir in flour. Blend well; then add milk and salt. Return to medium heat; stir constantly, until sauce is somewhat thickened. In a 3-quart glass casserole, layer potatoes with onions. Pour sauce over all. Cover and refrigerate.

*On Sabbath:* Sprinkle cheese over top of potatoes; bake at 350°F for 60 minutes.

## Layered Salad

Shredded iceberg lettuce
    (best if crisped beforehand)
Fresh mushrooms, sliced
Red onions, sliced

Frozen green peas (uncooked)
3/4 cup mayonnaise
3/4 teaspoon curry powder
Imitation bacon bits

Layer vegetables. Combine mayonnaise and curry powder; spread over top. Cover with plastic wrap; refrigerate for up to 24 hours. When ready to serve, mix well; sprinkle with bacon bits just before serving.

## Raspberry Cream Pie

*serves 8*

24 large marshmallows
1/3 cup milk
Pinch of salt
1 cup whipping cream, whipped,
    or 1 8-ounce container light whipped topping
1 9-inch baked pie shell
2 1-pint cartons raspberries

| PER SERVING | |
| --- | --- |
| CALORIES: | 308 |
| TOTAL FAT: | 18g |
| CHOLESTEROL: | 42mg |
| SODIUM: | 172mg |
| CARBOHYDRATE: | 36g |
| PROTEIN: | 3g |

Combine marshmallows, milk, and salt in a double boiler. Heat until marshmallows are melted. Cool. Fold in whipped cream or whipped topping. Put half of the marshmallow mixture in the bottom of the baked pie shell. Add most of the raspberries; top with rest of marshmallow cream. Garnish with remaining berries.

**Fresh Pea Soup**

*Waldorf Salad*

*Cornbread*

**Busy-Day Cake**

*Contributed by Luella Reile Johnson of San Diego, California*

*Luella says:* This simple meal is especially good in the wintertime. It is not rich, so you don't get the feeling of eating too much and being sleepy all afternoon. Our youngest son, Darren, helped us develop this recipe.

*Jackie says:* Luella knows how to serve a large crowd and create a simple, hospitable atmosphere with delicious, nutritious food! I'll always remember the Sabbath in the 1970s when she invited about 20 of us to her home in Loma Linda and served us a baked potato bar, with so many great toppings for the potatoes. It was the first time I had seen this done, and I was impressed! I knew she would contribute something special to our cookbook, and she has.

## Fresh Pea Soup

*serves 6*

1 tablespoon canola oil
2 cloves garlic, minced
2 medium onions, chopped
4 cups water
4 teaspoons chickenlike seasoning and broth mix

4 cups frozen peas
2 cups fresh spinach
Salt to taste
2 teaspoons butter-flavored seasoning

| PER SERVING | |
| --- | --- |
| CALORIES: | 124 |
| TOTAL FAT: | 3g |
| CHOLESTEROL: | 0mg |
| SODIUM: | 750mg |
| CARBOHYDRATE: | 20g |
| PROTEIN: | 6g |

Sauté garlic and onions in oil until transparent. Add water and chickenlike seasoning; bring to a boil. Add peas; cook 1 or 2 minutes, then add fresh spinach leaves. Cook 2 to 3 minutes more. Salt to taste; add butter seasoning. Put into a blender; purée/blend well.

*Luella says:* Make sure you do not overcook; this bright-green soup will darken if cooked too long. You may also use frozen spinach, but fresh is better. The soup may be made Thursday or Friday and reheated on Sabbath. Make sure you do not bring it to a boil or overcook when reheating, however.

## Waldorf Salad

*serves 6*

1 cup diced celery
1/2 cup chopped walnuts
1/2 cup raisins
3 cups diced Fuji apples
1 8-ounce carton light whipped topping

| PER SERVING | |
| --- | --- |
| CALORIES: | 234 |
| TOTAL FAT: | 11g |
| CHOLESTEROL: | 0mg |
| SODIUM: | 47mg |
| CARBOHYDRATE: | 31g |
| PROTEIN: | 3g |

*Luella says:* I dice the celery, measure the raisins, and chop the nuts, as well as wash the apples on Friday. Sabbath, I just cut the apples, add the other ingredients, toss, and serve.

## Busy-Day Cake

*serves 8*

*Luella says:* I like to serve this simple cake with this menu. My mother, Elsie Reile, used to make it for our family, and my sister, Carol Powers, also used this recipe in a cookbook she published some years ago.

1 1/3 cups flour
1 cup sugar
2 teaspoons baking powder
1/2 teaspoon salt
1/3 cup vegetable shortening

2/3 cup 2% milk
1 teaspoon vanilla
1 egg
Easy Broiled Frosting (recipe follows)

Combine flour, sugar, baking powder, and salt in a mixer bowl. Mix well; add shortening and milk. Beat for 2 minutes with an electric mixer on medium speed. Add vanilla and egg. Beat for 2 minutes more on medium speed. Pour batter into an 8" x 8" pan that has been greased and floured only on the bottom. Bake at 350°F for 30 to 35 minutes. Carefully spread frosting on the warm cake in the pan. Place cake with frosting under the broiler; broil until mixture is bubbly and golden brown. *Be careful not to burn!* Remove from oven; allow to cool.

## Easy Broiled Frosting

1/4 cup margarine
1/2 cup brown sugar
3 tablespoons whipping cream

3/4 cup flaked coconut
1/3 cup chopped pecans (optional)

Cream margarine and brown sugar. Mix well; add whipping cream. Mix well; add coconut and pecans. Mix all ingredients.

# SABBATH DINNER MENU #27

*Contributed by Dan Matthews of Thousand Oaks, California*

*Jackie says:* Until recently, Dan was the Speaker/Director and Program Production manager of the *Faith For Today* television program. Now retired, he has found a new career—that of being the chef at home. His wife Betsy is still employed, so Dan has the evening meal ready when she comes home from work, and Betsy says that it is wonderful. Dan has been experimenting with many recipes and has shared several of them with us. It was difficult to decide which ones to include!

**FriChik Almond Primavera**

**Pine Nut–Spinach Salad**

**French bread**

**Chilled seasonal fruit cup with homemade or store-bought cookies**

## FriChik Almond Primavera

*serves 4*

8 ounces whole-wheat fusilli pasta
1 medium red onion, thinly sliced
1 medium carrot, sliced diagonally
1 medium red bell pepper, julienned
1/2 pound snow peas
1 cup cauliflower florets
1/2 cup slivered almonds
2 cloves garlic, minced

2 teaspoons grated fresh ginger root
3 tablespoons extra-virgin olive oil
2 tablespoons soy sauce
1 12.5-ounce can Worthington® *Low-fat FriChik®*,
    cut into 1/2-inch slices
1 tablespoon lemon juice
Salt to taste

Cook pasta *al dente* in a large pot, or according to package instructions. Add vegetables, almonds, garlic, and ginger to oil and soy sauce in a large skillet. Simmer over medium heat for five minutes; add *FriChik®* and pasta. Stir in lemon juice and salt. Simmer, covered, for 5 to 7 more minutes.

*Dan says:* Be careful not to overcook the vegetables, and serve as soon as possible. This recipe makes a delicious one-dish meal to serve four people.

*Friday preparation:* All ingredients, including the pasta, can be prepared in advance and refrigerated. If you prepare the vegetables on Friday, cut them late in the afternoon so they will be as fresh as possible. With advance preparation, you should be able to cook this dish in about 15 minutes.

| PER SERVING | |
|---|---|
| CALORIES: | 538 |
| TOTAL FAT: | 26g |
| CHOLESTEROL: | 0mg |
| SODIUM: | 1074mg |
| CARBOHYDRATE: | 61g |
| PROTEIN: | 22g |

## Pine Nut-Spinach Salad

*serves 4*

1/4 cup lemon juice (fresh squeezed, if possible)
3/4 cup extra-virgin olive oil
Salt to taste
1 pound fresh spinach leaves
1/2 cup sliced white mushrooms
1 5-ounce can mandarin oranges
1/4 cup pine nuts

*Dressing:* Shake lemon juice and olive oil together well. Add salt to taste.

*Large spinach leaves may be torn into bite-size pieces.* Toss spinach, mushrooms, and mandarin oranges together in a large salad bowl. *If possible, serve on individual salad plates.* After arranging salad on each plate, sprinkle with pine nuts. Top each serving with approximately 1 tablespoon dressing, or to taste.

*Dan says:* This salad can be put together from ingredients prepared in advance, between stirrings of the FriChik Almond Primavera. If the table is set ahead of time, this entire menu—entree and salad, with rolls and beverage—could be on the table in less than 30 minutes.

**Gazpacho**

**Navy Bean–Tomato Bruschetta**

**Green Salad**

**Fresh Fruit Tart**

# SABBATH DINNER MENU #28

*Contributed by Connie Schlehuber Hunt and her three daughters,*
*Laura Hunt Ashlock, Alana Hunt Montes, and Sheri Hunt Bond*

*Jackie says:* The Schlehuber family were missionaries in Ceylon (now Sri Lanka) at the same time our family lived there. Their children—Connie, Shirley, and LaVerne—along with Lila and Lois Goertzen, and our children—Jeanne, Nancy, and Peter—enjoyed singing together. Their singing group, called "The Rusty Hinges," gave concerts in Colombo and even had their picture in the Colombo newspaper! Although the "children" are grown up and have families of their own, it is great to keep in touch.

*Connie says:* Sheri, Laura, Alana, and I have combined forces to come up with this menu and the recipes. So, it's a mother-and-her-three-daughters combo! How can you go wrong? The menu can be used for Friday supper or Sabbath lunch. This cool, refreshing meal is perfect for hot days when you don't want to heat the kitchen with the oven or stove. Both the bruschetta and the gazpacho can be made ahead of time and stored in the refrigerator.

## Gazpacho

*serves 4*

*Contributed by Sheri Hunt Bond of Greensboro, North Carolina*

3 or 4 tomatoes
1 small onion
2 cloves garlic
1 tablespoon fresh cilantro
1 1/2 teaspoons cumin powder
1 teaspoon Tabasco® sauce
1/4 teaspoon salt
1 1/4 cups canned black beans, drained
2 cups tomato juice
1/2 cup light sour cream

| PER SERVING | |
|---|---|
| CALORIES: | 131 |
| TOTAL FAT: | 1g |
| CHOLESTEROL: | 0mg |
| SODIUM: | 868mg |
| CARBOHYDRATE: | 25g |
| PROTEIN: | 7g |

In a food processor, combine tomatoes, onion, garlic, cilantro, cumin powder, Tabasco® sauce, and salt; blend well. Pour into a bowl; add black beans and tomato juice. Chill well; serve in soup bowls with a dollop of light sour cream.

## Navy Bean-Tomato Bruschetta

*serves 4*

*Contributed by Constance Schlehuber Hunt of Collegedale, Tennessee*

2 15-ounce cans navy beans, drained
1 ripe tomato, chopped
20 basil leaves, minced
1 ounce Feta cheese, crumbled
1 clove garlic, minced or crushed

1 tablespoon red onion, minced
1/2 teaspoon (or to taste) salt
1 tablespoon olive oil
2 tablespoons lemon juice
1 teaspoon sugar

| PER SERVING | |
| --- | --- |
| CALORIES: | 412 |
| TOTAL FAT: | 6g |
| CHOLESTEROL: | 6mg |
| SODIUM: | 363mg |
| CARBOHYDRATE: | 67g |
| PROTEIN: | 25g |

Mix ingredients well in a large bowl; chill. *To serve:* Place the bowl on a platter, surrounded by triangles of pita bread (French, rye, or whole grain bread can also be used). Diners can place the bruschetta on the bread themselves, or it can be served on the bread, arranged on a large platter.

## Green Salad

*serves 4*

*Contributed by Alana Hunt Montes of Healdsburg, California*

1 head red leaf lettuce, torn into bite-size pieces
1 head green leaf lettuce, torn into bite-size pieces

3 tomatoes, cut into wedges
1 avocado, cut into wedges

Combine lettuces; spread on salad plates. Arrange tomatoes and avocado wedges in a circular pattern on lettuce. Serve with balsamic vinaigrette or dressing of choice.

*Alana says:* This salad is best if made just before serving.

## Fresh Fruit Tart

*serves 8*

*Contributed by Laura Hunt Ashlock of Berrien Springs, Michigan*

| PER SERVING | |
|---|---|
| CALORIES: | 293 |
| TOTAL FAT: | 18g |
| CHOLESTEROL: | 55mg |
| SODIUM: | 359mg |
| CARBOHYDRATE: | 26g |
| PROTEIN: | 6g |

**Pastry**
1 1/2 cups flour
1/2 teaspoon salt
1/4 cup cold butter
1/4 cup vegetable shortening
4 tablespoons cold water

**Filling**
8 ounces light cream cheese, softened
1/4 cup sugar
1 egg
1 teaspoon vanilla
Seasonal fresh fruit

PASTRY: Combine flour and salt; cut in butter and shortening with a pastry blender. Add 4 tablespoons cold water slowly. Form into a flat disc; chill for 30 minutes. Roll on floured surface to fit the tart pan. Place in the pan, being careful not to stretch the dough. Press to sides; prick with a fork. Bake at 375°F for 10 to 12 minutes, until light brown and crisp.

FILLING: Mix cream cheese, sugar, egg, and vanilla well; spread mixture on the hot crust. Lower heat to 350°F; bake for 15 to 20 minutes. Remove and cool. About an hour before serving, arrange sliced fresh fruit on top in a circular pattern. *Suggested fruit options: strawberries, kiwi, raspberries, and mangoes.*

*Laura says:* This dessert can be made ahead. Do not add fresh fruit until 1 hour before serving. You will need an 11-inch tart pan that is 1 inch deep.

**Tender Homemade Gluten Chops**
**or Worthington® Choplets®**

**Creamed Peas**
**and New Potatoes**

*Salad of your choice*

*Whole-wheat bread or rolls*

**Iced Cranberry Tea**
**or sparkling grape juice**

**Piña Colada Delight**

# SABBATH DINNER MENU #29

*Contributed by T. Jean Voss-Peterson of Keene, Texas*

*Jackie says:* I've known Jean since we attended junior camp in Texas! That was a long time ago. It has been so nice to keep in touch through the years. These gluten steaks are the most tender and delicious ones I have ever eaten.

*Jean says:* I like to make my own gluten and have included a recipe, but for some it may be more practical to use the canned products. My sister-in-law, Evelyn Wilson, gave me her recipe, and now I have made it mine. I usually make a double batch, so I have plenty to put in the freezer. It always makes me feel good to know I can put a meal together quickly with something homemade. Just take the gluten chops out of the freezer and thaw in microwave for a few seconds so they will separate easily. Dip in flour and food yeast and brown in skillet.

## Tender Homemade Gluten Chops

*serves 10*

1 1/2 teaspoon onion powder
1 teaspoon salt
3 tablespoons brewer's yeast
1 tablespoon soy flour
1/2 cup all-purpose flour
2 cups gluten flour
1 2/3 cups water
3 tablespoons soy sauce

**Broth**

3 quarts water
1 whole onion
2 stalks celery
2 tablespoons garlic powder
1 tablespoon Vegex®, Savorex®, or Marmite®
1/2 cup soy sauce
1 tablespoon Accent® (optional)

Mix onion powder, salt, yeast, and flour in a large bowl; add water and soy sauce. Mix well, getting all of the liquid worked into the flour mixture. *This happens fast!* Shape into a 12-inch roll; slice 1/2-inch thick to make chops or steaks. Combine broth ingredients; bring to a boil. Flatten with fingers and drop slices carefully into boiling broth. Cover; gently simmer over medium heat for 45 minutes.

When finished, lift chops into a shallow dish to cool. Mix equal parts flour and brewer's yeast; coat the chops well on both sides. Fry in a small amount of olive oil. *Freeze the remaining steaks for future use. Using a quart-sized plastic freezer bag, put four steaks, stacked in twos, into the bag without any added broth. These freeze well.* Strain the broth to use for gravy.

*Note: If using Worthington® Choplets® for your entree, mix equal parts flour and brewer's yeast; coat the chops well on both sides. Fry in a small amount of olive oil.*

| PER SERVING (HOMEMADE CHOPS) | |
|---|---|
| CALORIES: | 37 |
| TOTAL FAT: | >1g |
| CHOLESTEROL: | 0mg |
| SODIUM: | 526mg |
| CARBOHYDRATE: | 7g |
| PROTEIN: | 2g |

## Creamed Peas and New Potatoes

*serves 8*

16 small new red potatoes
1 16-ounce package frozen petite peas
Packaged cream gravy, prepared, or homemade cream sauce

*Jean says:* I scrape and parboil the potatoes on Friday and refrigerate in a sealed plastic bag. On Sabbath, I bring the potatoes to a boil, and cook until done. Add fresh or frozen peas the last 8 to 10 minutes. Use a packaged cream gravy or make your own cream sauce and pour over the drained vegetables when transferring to the serving bowl.

## Iced Cranberry Tea

Make a pitcher of herbal or decaffeinated tea; add lemon and sugar to taste. Just before serving, add cranberry juice to taste. Serve in tall glasses over crushed ice.

*Jean's Hostess Tip:* I keep 2 or 3 bottles of Martinelli's® sparkling red grape drink in the refrigerator for a quick company drink. Serve cold in shallow stemware glasses.

## Piña Colada Delight

*serves 15*

1 box yellow cake mix, baked as directed*
1 14-ounce can sweetened condensed milk
1 10-ounce can frozen Piña Colada mix, thawed (do not dilute)
1 8-ounce carton light whipped topping
1/2 cup shredded or flaked coconut

| PER SERVING | |
|---|---|
| CALORIES: | 340 |
| TOTAL FAT: | 10g |
| CHOLESTEROL: | 10mg |
| SODIUM: | 285mg |
| CARBOHYDRATE: | 58g |
| PROTEIN: | 4g |

Bake the cake in a 9" x 13" pan on Thursday or Friday. Poke holes in the top of the cake with a fork while the cake is still very hot. Combine sweetened condensed milk and Piña Colada mix; spread over the cake. Let cool to room temperature. When the topping has soaked in and the cake is cool, cover and refrigerate. The morning you plan to serve the cake, spread whipped topping over the top and sprinkle with coconut. Refrigerate; serve cold.

*\* Pineapple or orange flavored cake mix can be substituted for yellow cake mix.*

**Fettucine With Almond-Zucchini Sauce**

**Broccoli Delight With Zesty Horseradish Topping**

*Tossed salad with vegetables of your choice*

**Olives**

**White Cake With Vanilla Sauce**

# SABBATH DINNER MENU #30

*Contributed by Kathy Huey of Portland, Oregon*

*Jackie says:* Kathy is always coming up with some unique recipe. Be sure to try her Broccoli Delight With Zesty Horseradish Topping. It is delicious!

*Kathy says:* I have served this fettuccine dish for many years, and our guests have always enjoyed it. The White Cake With Vanilla Sauce was a favorite of my mother when I was growing up. So it's been a favorite of mine for longer than I want to tell!

## Fettuccine w/Almond-Zucchini Sauce

*serves 8*

| PER SERVING | |
|---|---|
| CALORIES: | 307 |
| TOTAL FAT: | 8g |
| CHOLESTEROL: | 12mg |
| SODIUM: | 527mg |
| CARBOHYDRATE: | 51g |
| PROTEIN: | 10g |

3 tablespoons butter
3 cups sliced zucchini
1 large onion, chopped
1 clove garlic, minced
2 8-ounce cans tomato sauce
$1/2$ teaspoon dry oregano

$1/4$ teaspoon dry rosemary
$1/4$ teaspoon red pepper flakes
$1/2$ teaspoon salt
1 teaspoon sugar
1 pound fettucine, cooked *al dente*
Toasted sliced almonds

Sauté zucchini, onion, and garlic in melted butter until tender. Add tomato sauce and seasonings. Simmer until hot and thoroughly combined.

Serve noodles on a platter. Pass the sauce and let guests serve themselves. Top with almonds.

*Kathy says:* This recipe can all be made on Friday. The fettuccini can be cooked ahead. Put a pot of hot water on to boil when you arrive home from church, drop the cooked fettucine into the rapidly boiling water for 2 or 3 minutes, drain, and it is ready to serve.

## Broccoli Delight With Zesty Horseradish Topping

*serves 10*

1 1/2 pounds broccoli
2/3 cup light sour cream
2/3 cup light mayonnaise

2 teaspoons prepared mustard
1 teaspoon lemon juice
1/2 tablespoon horseradish

| PER SERVING | |
|---|---|
| CALORIES: | 44 |
| TOTAL FAT: | 3g |
| CHOLESTEROL: | 7mg |
| SODIUM: | 97mg |
| CARBOHYDRATE: | 3g |
| PROTEIN: | >1g |

Steam broccoli until tender. Meanwhile, combine sour cream, mayonnaise, mustard, lemon juice, and horseradish in a small saucepan; heat over low heat until warm. Transfer to a serving container; pass as a topping for the broccoli.

## White Cake With Vanilla Sauce

*serves 8*

1 box white cake mix

Vanilla Sauce (recipe follows)

Bake cake in 9" x 13" baking dish according to directions on the box. Place slices of cake on dessert plates; spoon warm Vanilla Sauce over the cake just before serving.

| PER SERVING | |
|---|---|
| CALORIES: | 82 |
| TOTAL FAT: | 3g |
| CHOLESTEROL: | 8mg |
| SODIUM: | 97mg |
| CARBOHYDRATE: | 14g |
| PROTEIN: | >1g |

## Vanilla Sauce

1/2 cup sugar
2 tablespoons flour
1/4 teaspoon salt

1 cup boiling water
2 tablespoons butter
1 teaspoon vanilla

Mix sugar, flour, and salt; add boiling water, stirring constantly. Boil until clear. Remove from heat; add butter and vanilla. Serve warm.

# SABBATH DINNER MENU #31

*Edna Johnson Abrams of College Place, Washington*

*Edna says:* We were recently invited to Sabbath dinner by two young women who had just returned from a trip overseas. Our hostesses explained that the entree is called "African Delight." I looked at the assortment of foods and thought to myself, *Instead of being an African **delight**, I think this is going to be an African **experience!*** Because there was nothing else to eat, I had no choice but to try it. When it came to adding raisins to the combination, I hesitated; however, I decided to add them to the entree—and to my surprise, it tasted good! My husband Paul also had misgivings, but he liked it too. So, my advice to you is, Be brave and try the recipe! I think you will agree, this will be an "African Delight"!

*Jackie says:* When Edna first told me about this entree, I couldn't imagine the combination either. But, it looked like a fun dinner. We served it when we were on a camping trip; some in the group liked it, and some didn't. But we had fun trying it!

African Delight

Orange gelatin salad

Cranberry Mayonnaise Cake

## African Delight

*serves 8*

4 cups rice, cooked according to directions ($1/2$ cup rice per person)
1 can black olives, chopped
2 apples, chopped
2 or 3 bananas, chopped
2 or 3 oranges, peeled and chopped
1 cup raisins
1 or 2 avocados, chopped
1 cup unsweetened shredded coconut
1 20-ounce can pineapple tidbits
2 32-ounce cans tomato soup, ready to serve from the can
1 tablespoon (or to taste) curry powder
1 cup Virginia peanuts, toasted brown and crushed

*Edna says:* In the African culture, the more affluent families serve many toppings. You may serve all these toppings, or you may choose to serve only a few of them.

Prepare the toppings; put each in a small bowl. Place rice at the beginning of the lineup. Heat tomato soup; add curry powder. Place soup at the end of the lineup of toppings.

Begin by putting about $1/2$ cup of hot rice on your plate. Then top with about 1 to 2 tablespoons of each side dish. Use a soup ladle to spoon the hot tomato soup over all, using 1/3 cup of soup per serving. Finally, top with toasted peanuts. *Enjoy! This will be a nice African experience, and it is vegan!*

## Cranberry Mayonnaise Cake

*serves 10*

3 cups unsifted flour
1 cup sugar
2 teaspoons baking soda
1 teaspoon salt
1 cup light mayonnaise
1 cup chopped nuts
1 16-ounce can whole berry cranberry sauce (reserve $1/4$ cup)
Grated rind of 1 orange
$1/2$ cup orange juice
Cranberry Frosting (recipe follows)

Mix all ingredients (except reserved cranberry sauce and frosting). Pour into a 9" x 3 $1/2$" tube pan lined with greased waxed paper. Bake at 350°F for about 75 minutes, or until cake tester inserted in center comes out clean. Remove from the pan. When cool, frost with Cranberry Frosting.

| PER SERVING | |
|---|---|
| CALORIES: | 552 |
| TOTAL FAT: | 16g |
| CHOLESTEROL: | 9mg |
| SODIUM: | 648mg |
| CARBOHYDRATE: | 97g |
| PROTEIN: | 6g |

## Cranberry Frosting

3 tablespoons margarine
2 cups powdered sugar
$1/4$ cup reserved cranberry sauce

Beat until creamy.

**Creamy Chicken Rice Casserole**

**Frozen cut corn**

**Creamed petite peas**

**Tossed salad**

**Olives**

**Rolls, butter, and jam**

**Sugarless Apple Pie**

# SABBATH DINNER MENU #32

*Contributed by Edna Harris of Portland, Oregon*

*Edna says:* This rice casserole is special to me. When I returned home after a week in the hospital, my second-cousin brought us a large bowl of this casserole, unbaked. Each day Jack and I baked just enough for one meal. It lasted all week and is a wonderful, nutritious main dish. This recipe may seem complicated, but it really is not. It is so easy to make and can be made a day or two in advance. It keeps well in the refrigerator, or may even be frozen after it has been baked. Trust me, it is worth all you put into it!

*Jackie says:* This Creamy Chicken Rice Casserole is absolutely delicious and has become one of my favorites.

## Creamy Chicken Rice Casserole

*serves 8*

1 cup uncooked rice
1/2 cup margarine
1/2 cup chopped onion
1/4 cup flour
1 6-ounce can (1 1/3 cups) broiled, sliced mushrooms (reserve liquid)
1 tablespoon chickenlike seasoning and broth mix
1 1/2 cups 2% milk or half-and-half

1 12.5-ounce can Worthington® FriChik®, drained and cubed
1/4 cup diced pimentos
2 tablespoons snipped dried parsley
1 teaspoon salt
1/2 teaspoon seasoned salt
1 cup blanched, slivered almonds (optional)

| PER SERVING | |
| --- | --- |
| CALORIES: | 384 |
| TOTAL FAT: | 25g |
| CHOLESTEROL: | 3mg |
| SODIUM: | 891mg |
| CARBOHYDRATE: | 30g |
| PROTEIN: | 11g |

Prepare rice according to package directions; set aside. Cook onion in margarine over low heat till tender, but not brown (about 10 minutes); remove from heat. Stir in flour; set aside. Using reserved mushroom liquid, add enough water to measure 1 1/2 cups. Add chickenlike seasoning. Mix well; stir into flour mixture. Add half-and-half or milk; stir until mixture thickens.

To the cooked rice add mushrooms, *FriChik*®, pimentos, parsley, and salt. If using slivered almonds, add 1/2 cup to the mixture to be baked. Place in a 2-quart casserole; sprinkle with remaining 1/2 cup almonds. *It is good with or without the nuts.* If mixture seems too thick, use a bit more liquid, such as milk or cream. Cover; bake at 350°F for about 30 minutes. Remove cover 5 to 10 minutes before removing from oven to crisp the nuts.

## Sugarless Apple Pie

See recipe on p. 99 of the *Sabbath Dinner Cookbook.*

**Vareniki**
**(Russian Cheese Pockets)**

**Wild-Rice Casserole**

**Tossed salad**

**Pumpkin pie**

# SABBATH DINNER MENU #33

*Contributed by Van Haas of College Place, Washington*

*Jackie says:* If your grandmother used to make Vareniki and you've lost the recipe, here it is! When Van married her husband Elmer, she went to live in North Dakota with all the wonderful German cooks, many of whom had come from Russia and Ukraine.

*Kristi says:* When I was living in Ukraine, my friends told me that Vareniki is considered to be the Ukrainian national dish. They can make the cheese filling salty or sweet, depending on whether they want to use it for a main dish or for dessert. They also vary the fillings, using burger, onions, and cabbage; potatoes; or fruit, such as cherries. When Vareniki is served as a main dish, it is often topped with sautéed garlic and onions; but, sweet or salty, it is *always* topped with *smetana* (sour cream)! I haven't had Vareniki since I left Ukraine because most of my friends there did not have the instructions written down, and I have hesitated to try to make it myself. I'm thrilled to finally have a good recipe to use so that I can make this delicious dish that brings back so many cherished memories and share it with my American friends and family!

## Vareniki (Russian Cheese Pockets)

*serves 10*

**Filling**
1 egg, beaten
1/4 teaspoon salt
1 tablespoon cream cheese
1 pound dry-curd cottage cheese

**Dough**
1 egg, beaten
1 tablespoon oil
1/2 cup water + 2 tablespoons 2% or skim milk
1/4 teaspoon salt
2 1/2 cups sifted white flour

**Sauce**
1 pint half-and-half
Salt to taste
Seasoning salt to taste

| PER SERVING | |
| --- | --- |
| CALORIES: | 238 |
| TOTAL FAT: | 9g |
| CHOLESTEROL: | 60mg |
| SODIUM: | 150mg |
| CARBOHYDRATE: | 25g |
| PROTEIN: | 14g |

FILLING: Blend salt and cream cheese with egg. Add cottage cheese; mix well. Place in a pan; press down.

DOUGH: Add oil, diluted milk, and salt to egg. Add flour; knead well. *If dough is a little too soft, add more flour.* Roll out dough; cut with a 3-inch cookie cutter or a glass with a wide rim (larger ones are easier to work with). Dip finger into water; apply around the edge of the circle so edges will seal well. Place 1 teaspoon of cheese filling into each circle of dough (if using a larger cutter, use more filling). Fold edges over; pinch together to seal. When finished, lay cheese pockets on waxed paper that has been sprayed with cooking spray, so they will not stick together.

Drop Vareniki into boiling water; cook about 2 minutes. Remove one by one from the boiling water; spray both sides with cooking spray. Place in a baking dish; cover with half-and-half that has

## Vareniki (continued)

been seasoned with salt and seasoning salt. Bake in 350°F oven for 30 to 45 minutes, so cream is partially absorbed.

*Note: Vareniki can be made ahead of time and frozen for later use. After boiling them, cool and then freeze them in layers separated by waxed paper. Then you can take out just as many as you need, put them in boiling water just long enough to heat through, and then place in a casserole with seasoned half-and-half.*

## Wild-Rice Casserole

*serves 8*

1 cup wild rice
1 tablespoon butter or margarine
1 onion, chopped fine
1 29-ounce can stewed tomatoes
1 4-ounce can sliced mushrooms, drained
1 8-ounce can tomato sauce
1/2 pound Longhorn or imitation Cheddar cheese, grated
1/4 pound Swiss cheese, grated

| PER SERVING | |
|---|---|
| CALORIES: | 297 |
| TOTAL FAT: | 15g |
| CHOLESTEROL: | 43mg |
| SODIUM: | 430mg |
| CARBOHYDRATE: | 27g |
| PROTEIN: | 16g |

Wash rice thoroughly several times. Sauté onion in butter. Combine all ingredients; pour into a 9" x 13" casserole. Cover with aluminum foil; bake at 250°F for 3 hours. Remove cover during the last 15 minutes of baking.

# Sabbath Dinner Menu #34

*Contributed by June Pfaff of College Place, Washington*

*June says:* On Friday I make the patties, Rhubarb Dessert, and the Marinated Garden Tomatoes. My Irish mother used to make these special baked potatoes, although she used butter. But I find that the olive oil works better. We can't get our fill of these potatoes. They are even good cold!

*Jackie says:* When I first moved to College Place, someone told me that June Pfaff was "the best cook in town." I was anxious to meet her and so pleased that she contributed a menu for this cookbook. Her Bulgur-Wheat Patties are delicious, as are the Irish Baked Potatoes. We enjoy the Marinated Garden Tomatoes too. What a great way to use some of the tomatoes from your summer garden! You'll enjoy her complete menu.

**Bulgur-Wheat Patties**

**Irish Baked Potatoes**

**Marinated Garden Tomatoes**

**Sweet Pea Pods**

**Rhubarb Dessert**

## Bulgur-Wheat Patties

*makes 16 patties*

1/2 cup bulgur wheat
1 cup water
2 medium onions, chopped
3/4 cup chopped walnuts or pecans
2 cups grated light or fat-free processed cheese
  (refrigerate first)
1 cup crushed herb-seasoned stuffing
1 teaspoon garlic salt
4 eggs or 1 cup Morningstar Farms® Scramblers®
1 package onion soup mix
2 cups boiling water

In a pan, combine bulgur wheat with 1 cup water; bring to a boil. Lower heat; cover and simmer 10 minutes. Remove from heat; let stand till cooled.

Place onion in a microwave-safe dish; cover. Sauté in the microwave, without water, 2 to 3 minutes.

In a large bowl, combine nuts, cheese, stuffing, and garlic salt. Add bulgur wheat, sautéed onions, and eggs. *If too soft, can add 1/2 cup Italian seasoned bread crumbs.* Mix well; form into 16 patties. Place in a 9" x 13" casserole, cover with plastic wrap; refrigerate.

*Sabbath morning:* Mix onion soup mix with 2 cups boiling water; pour over patties. Cover; bake at 350°F for 60 minutes. *I set the automatic oven to come on so that these should be finished about 15 minutes before we plan to eat Sabbath dinner. These can bake with the potatoes.*

## Irish Baked Potatoes

*serves 8*

I choose 8 to 10 large red potatoes, wash them well, and cut in half lengthwise. Dry; rub all over with olive oil. Salt the cut side; lay halves on an oiled cookie sheet (or smaller pan) with the cut side down. Sprinkle with salt; bake, uncovered, at 350°F for 60 minutes. *They should be crispy and brown on the cut side. You may have to grease the pan with some olive oil also.*

## Marinated Garden Tomatoes

*serves 10*

*June says:* These Marinated Garden Tomatoes are so good when tomatoes are in season. You can make this recipe a day ahead, since the tomatoes can marinate overnight. Men seem to especially enjoy this recipe.

| PER SERVING | |
| --- | --- |
| CALORIES: | 84 |
| TOTAL FAT: | 7g |
| CHOLESTEROL: | 0mg |
| SODIUM: | 222mg |
| CARBOHYDRATE: | 5g |
| PROTEIN: | 1g |

1/3 cup olive or canola oil
1/4 cup lemon juice
   or red-wine or cider vinegar
1/4 cup minced fresh
   or 1 tablespoon dried parsley
2 cloves garlic, finely minced

1 teaspoon salt
1 tablespoon snipped fresh
   or 1 teaspoon dried thyme
6 large tomatoes, cut into wedges
1/2 cup thinly sliced green onions

Combine oil, lemon juice or vinegar, parsley, garlic, salt, and thyme. Place tomatoes and green onions in a bowl; cover with marinade. Cover; refrigerate at least 2 hours or overnight. *Marinade can be reused several times.*

## Sweet Pea Pods

*serves 8*

*June says:* This Sweet Pea Pod recipe was given to me by a close friend many years ago, and it has always been my favorite vegetable, especially for Sabbath dinner. I purchase them in season from the Schwan® salesman.

1 16-ounce package sweet pea pods
1/4 cup minced onions

Nonfat liquid margarine
Salt to taste

Steam the package of sweet pea pods in a double boiler, till done but still crisp. Put in a bowl; add onion and spray with nonfat liquid margarine. Salt to taste.

## Rhubarb Dessert

*serves 15*

*June says:* A dear friend in North Dakota shared this recipe with me years ago, and we always love to make it, especially when rhubarb is in season.

**Crust**
2 1/2 cups graham cracker crumbs
1/3 cup sugar
1/2 cup reduced-fat margarine
    or melted butter

**First layer**
3/4 cups water
1 1/2 cups sugar
5 tablespoons cornstarch
6 cups sliced rhubarb
1 3-ounce package strawberry gelatin

**Second Layer**
1 8-ounce container light
    or fat-free whipped topping
2 cups miniature marshmallows

**Third Layer**
1 3.4-ounce package instant
    lemon pudding mix
2 cups cold skim milk
Chopped nuts

CRUST: Combine ingredients; press into a 9" x 13" cake pan. Either chill 5 to 10 minutes before filling or bake at 375°F for 6 to 8 minutes for a crispier texture. Cool.

FIRST LAYER: Mix water, sugar, cornstarch, and rhubarb; cook until thick. Remove from heat; add strawberry gelatin. Mix well; cool completely. Spread onto graham-cracker crust.

SECOND LAYER: Mix whipped topping and marshmallows. Mix well; spread over rhubarb filling.

THIRD LAYER: Mix pudding mix with cold skim milk. When thickened somewhat, spread over the whipped topping and marshmallow layer. Sprinkle chopped nuts over the top. Cover and chill in the refrigerator at least 8 hours. *I chill this dessert overnight.*

# Sabbath Dinner Menu #35

*Contributed by Joseph Blahovich of Vancouver, Washington*

*Kristi says:* I have been so lucky to have had Joseph and Frances as a part of my life from before I was even a part of it! They actually catered my parents' wedding reception, and I recently came across a recipe from that meal that I had painstakingly recopied when working toward my baking honor as a fifth grader in Pathfinders.

Frances created the wonderful enrichment program at my elementary school, and from her program we had many of our first experiences with computers, art, critical thinking, and cultural awareness. Every year chef Joseph would treat all the students to his famous homemade pizza—my favorite was his Hawaiian pizza topped with pineapple and *Stripples*®. When I was in college and too far away to go home for Thanksgiving, they welcomed me and my friends to their home, making us part of their family for the holiday. I'm only one of hundreds of "Blahovich kids" who have been blessed by their hospitality and by the love around their table where there is always room for one or two more.

*Joseph says:* This menu is for a group of 25 to 30 people.

**Swiss Steaks, Vegetarian Style**

**Garlic Parsley Potatoes**

**Green Vegetable Stir-Fry**

**Spinach Kiwi Salad**

*Bread of your choice*

**Kellogg's Corn Flakes Drops**

2 cups all-purpose flour seasoned with
    garlic powder and seasoned salt (for breading)
5 20-ounce cans Worthington® *Multi-grain Cutlets*®
    or Loma Linda® *Dinner Cuts*®
1 1/4 cups + 2 tablespoons olive oil, divided
1 pound fresh mushrooms, sliced
2 large green peppers, diced
3 large onions (1 1/2 pounds), diced
1 4-ounce jar diced pimiento

**Gravy**

3/4 cup olive or canola oil
1 1/2 cups all-purpose flour
12 cups water
6 heaping tablespoons (or to taste) chickenlike
    seasoning and broth mix
1 1/2 teaspoons browning and seasoning sauce
3 tablespoons soy sauce
1 tablespoon seasoning salt

*Friday preparation:* Roll cutlets in flour seasoned with garlic salt and seasoned salt to taste. Sauté cutlets in 1 1/4 cups olive oil, till lightly browned. Sauté mushrooms, peppers, and onion in remaining 2 tablespoons olive oil*; add pimiento. In large glass baking dishes, arrange cutlets in three rows, at 45-degree angles, slightly overlapping each other. Add sautéed veggies. Cover with plastic wrap; place in the refrigerator.

GRAVY: In a large kettle, combine oil and flour; simmer until golden brown. Remove from heat; add water, stirring constantly. Return to heat; stir until thickened. Boil 1 minute; add seasonings. Continue simmering 5 to 10 minutes, stirring often. Cool, cover, and place in the refrigerator.

*Sabbath morning:* Heat gravy in the microwave or stovetop, stirring often, and pour over the cutlets, making sure each one is covered. Bake at 350° F for 90 minutes.

*\*Note: To reduce calories, sauté the veggies in water or microwave until tender. Any type of vegetarian cutlets may be used for this recipe.*

| PER SERVING | |
| --- | --- |
| CALORIES: | 246 |
| TOTAL FAT: | 16g |
| CHOLESTEROL: | 0mg |
| SODIUM: | 965mg |
| CARBOHYDRATE: | 14g |
| PROTEIN: | 13g |

## Garlic Parsley Potatoes

*serves 30*

6 pounds small red potatoes
1 cup chopped fresh parsley
1 cup chopped fresh chives
10 to 12 garlic cloves, minced
2 cubes (1 cup) margarine
1 tablespoon salt
Morningstar Farms® *Breakfast Strips*®, fried and crumbled (optional)

| PER SERVING | |
|---|---|
| CALORIES: | 147 |
| TOTAL FAT: | 8g |
| CHOLESTEROL: | 0mg |
| SODIUM: | 357mg |
| CARBOHYDRATE: | 18g |
| PROTEIN: | 3g |

*Friday preparation:* Wash and boil potatoes for 15 to 20 minutes, until tender. Drain and cut in half. Place parsley, chives, and garlic, and salt in individual small bowls.

In a large skillet, melt half a cube (1/4 cup) margarine. Add 1/4 of the parsley, chives, and garlic. Cook and stir over medium heat for 5 minutes. Add 1/4 of the potatoes; sprinkle with 1 teaspoon salt. Toss to coat for about 5 minutes. Continue preparing the three remaining portions of the ingredients as above. Place in a casserole. Sprinkle with *Breakfast Strips*® if desired.

*On Sabbath:* Place casserole in the oven; bake at 350°F until lightly browned, approximately 45 minutes.

## Green Vegetable Stir-Fry

*serves 30*

3 pounds broccoli
4 pounds fresh asparagus
2 pounds snow peas
3 cups water, divided

3 teaspoons salt, divided
3 teaspoons chickenlike seasoning
   and broth mix, divided

*Friday preparation:* Wash and cut vegetables; place in individual bowls. Cover tightly and refrigerate.

*On Sabbath:* Combine broccoli, asparagus, and snow peas in a large bowl. Divide vegetables into thirds. Stir-fry each batch on high heat for 3 minutes, adding 1 cup water, 1 teaspoon salt, and 1 teaspoon chickenstyle seasoning to each of the batches as you cook them. Serve immediately.

## Spinach Kiwi Salad

*serves 30*

2 bags (3 pounds) spinach
6 kiwi, peeled and sliced
1 large (mild) onion, peeled and sliced and cut in half
1 quart firm fresh raspberries
1 pound blanched, slivered almonds
1 box herb seasoned croutons
1 cup grated Parmesan cheese (optional)

| PER SERVING | |
| --- | --- |
| CALORIES: | 136 |
| TOTAL FAT: | 9g |
| CHOLESTEROL: | 2mg |
| SODIUM: | 104mg |
| CARBOHYDRATE: | 10g |
| PROTEIN: | 6g |

Wash and drain spinach (if needed); place in a large bowl. Peel and slice kiwi and onion; add to spinach. Toss gently to mix. Top with raspberries, almonds, croutons, and Parmesan, if desired. Serve with raspberry salad dressing or dressing of your choice.

## Kellogg's Corn Flakes Drops

*makes 6 dozen*

1 cup light corn syrup
$^1/_2$ cup sugar
1 cup peanut butter (old-fashioned, not hydrogenated)
1 teaspoon vanilla
5 cups Kellogg's® *Corn Flakes*® cereal

In a large saucepan (3 or 4 quarts), bring corn syrup and sugar to boiling. Add peanut butter; remove from heat. Stir well. Stir in vanilla and *Corn Flakes®;* mix well. Drop by a small scoop or heaping teaspoon onto waxed paper or aluminum foil; store in an airtight plastic bowl. *These may be served with a dish of berries or any kind of fruit or ice cream.*

**Smoked-Turkey Roast**

**Baked potatoes**

**Savory Carrots**

**Green peas**

**Cranberry sauce**

**Salad of your choice**

**Whole-wheat rolls**

**Lime Pie**

# SABBATH DINNER MENU #36

*Contributed by Jackie Beck of College Place, Washington*

*Jackie says:* This Smoked-Turkey Roast has been our family favorite for at least thirty years. We prepare it as our Thanksgiving or Christmas entree, and we all enjoy it. It freezes well too. You can also use the Chicken Roll in place of the Smoked Turkey.

I like to set the table Friday afternoon or Sabbath morning before leaving for church so it is ready when company comes for Sabbath dinner. I use my special china and silverware for Sabbath and like to put together a pretty centerpiece for the table. Even a simple arrangement of fresh flowers is pretty. This makes Sabbath special, and I am a more relaxed hostess.

## Smoked-Turkey Roast

*serves 15*

1 cup finely chopped onions
1 cup finely chopped celery
32 ounces (approximately 4 cups grated)
    Worthington® *Meatless Smoked Turkey*®,
    thawed at room temperature
1 teaspoon seasoned salt
1/2 cup seasoned bread stuffing
1/2 cup soda cracker crumbs

1/2 teaspoon poultry seasoning
1/2 teaspoon dried basil
2 teaspoons chickenlike seasoning and broth mix
3 tablespoons melted margarine
1 cup evaporated milk
3 eggs, beaten or 3/4 cup Morningstar Farms®
    *Scramblers*®
1 cup water

Sauté onion and celery in margarine over medium-low heat. Cut turkey roll into sections; grate in the food processor or by hand. Mix seasoned salt, stuffing, cracker crumbs, poultry seasoning, basil, chickenlike seasoning, and melted margarine. Blend well; add grated turkey. Add sautéed onions and celery. Mix evaporated milk, eggs, and water; pour over other ingredients, mixing well. Press into a greased 9" x 13" casserole. Cover and refrigerate.

*Sabbath morning:* Remove roast from the refrigerator; set in a pan of water. *Set the oven timer so roast will be finished baking by the time you return from church.* Bake, uncovered, at 350°F for 45 minutes. Let set about five minutes. Then, cut into thirds lengthwise, and into fifths crosswise. Using a spatula, lift each section out of the baking dish and onto a platter. Garnish with parsley; serve.

| PER SERVING | |
|---|---|
| CALORIES: | 242 |
| TOTAL FAT: | 15g |
| CHOLESTEROL: | 42mg |
| SODIUM: | 1006mg |
| CARBOHYDRATE: | 13g |
| PROTEIN: | 14g |

## Savory Carrots

*serves 8*

*Jackie says:* A friend, Jan Hoffman, shared this recipe with me years ago.

5 cups sliced carrots
1 cup light sour cream
1 3-ounce package light cream cheese
3 tablespoons minced green pepper

1/2 teaspoon salt
1/2 teaspoon lemon zest
2 tablespoons sliced green onion

| PER SERVING | |
|---|---|
| CALORIES: | 69 |
| TOTAL FAT: | 3g |
| CHOLESTEROL: | 8mg |
| SODIUM: | 227mg |
| CARBOHYDRATE: | 10g |
| PROTEIN: | 3g |

Cook carrots until just tender, but still bright in color; drain well. In another saucepan, combine remaining ingredients; heat through. Combine with carrots; serve.

## Lime Pie

*serves 8*

*Jackie says:* When we lived overseas, we could not get lemons, but limes were available. I still prefer using limes when I make this pie. It is one of our family favorites.

1/3 cup cornstarch
1 1/2 cups sugar
1/4 teaspoon salt
1 1/2 cups water
4 egg yolks, slightly beaten

1/2 cup fresh lime juice
1 tablespoon lime zest
2 tablespoons butter or margarine
1 9-inch baked pie shell
1 8-ounce container light whipped topping

| PER SERVING | |
|---|---|
| CALORIES: | 396 |
| TOTAL FAT: | 15g |
| CHOLESTEROL: | 106mg |
| SODIUM: | 272mg |
| CARBOHYDRATE: | 61g |
| PROTEIN: | 3g |

Combine cornstarch, sugar, and salt. Add water, stirring till smooth; boil 1 minute. Stir half the filling mixture into beaten egg yolks. When well blended, return to the pan; stir into the other half of the filling. Boil 1 minute. Remove from heat; stir in lime juice, zest, and butter. Pour immediately into cooled pie crust, top with whipped topping. *We prefer to use whipped topping instead of meringue.*

# SABBATH DINNER MENU #37

*Contributed by Peggy Stevenson Gray of Boise, Idaho*

*Peggy says:* This rice-and-curry dish is easy and yummy. Emma Olson, a hospitable church member, shared this recipe when Jim pastored the Rapid City church in South Dakota many years ago.

*Jackie says:* Peggy and I have been friends since we were in junior camp together—more years ago than we'd like to admit! We have always kept in touch through the years.

Rice and Curry

Green peas

Skillet Corn

Peggy's Coleslaw

Whole-wheat rolls

Microwave Apple Crisp

Lemonade With Lemonade
   Ice Cubes

## Rice and Curry

*serves 8*

2 cups brown or white rice, uncooked
1/2 teaspoon salt (optional)

**Curry**
1/4 cup + 2 teaspoons margarine, divided
2 cups chopped onion
1 teaspoon curry powder

2 cans 10.75-ounce condensed
   cream of mushroom soup, undiluted
1 soup can milk
8 eggs or 2 cups Morningstar Farms®
   Scramblers®
1/8 teaspoon salt
1/2 cup toasted cashews

Cook rice according to package directions.

Sauté onion in 1/4 cup margarine till tender. Add curry powder; cook on low for 3 to 4 minutes. Thin mushroom soup with milk, or to gravy consistency; add to the onion mixture. Beat eggs; add salt. Scramble in 2 teaspoons margarine till golden, stirring continually until dry and in small pieces. Add to mushroom soup mixture; mix well. Add cashews if desired. Serve over rice.

*Jackie says:* This curry is delicious! It reminded us of a special meal we used to eat when we were missionaries in Burma (now called Myanmar), years ago. It was called *Kausswei* and is pronounced "cow-sway." When serving this curry, to make it like *Kausswei,* serve it over rice sticks or spaghetti. Chop onions and cilantro leaves. Place the cooked rice sticks (maifun noodles) or spaghetti on your plate, spoon *Kausswei* over the spaghetti, and top with onion and cilantro leaves. Enjoy your Burmese meal. Yum!!!

| PER SERVING | |
| --- | --- |
| CALORIES: | 421 |
| TOTAL FAT: | 19g |
| CHOLESTEROL: | 190mg |
| SODIUM: | 826mg |
| CARBOHYDRATE: | 50g |
| PROTEIN: | 13g |

## Skillet Corn

*serves 8*

1 15-ounce can whole-kernel corn, drained
1/2 cup light cream or milk
Salt to taste
Sugar to taste
1 tablespoon margarine

| PER SERVING | |
| --- | --- |
| CALORIES: | 37 |
| TOTAL FAT: | 2g |
| CHOLESTEROL: | 1mg |
| SODIUM: | 27mg |
| CARBOHYDRATE: | 4g |
| PROTEIN: | 1g |

In a skillet, heat corn with cream, adding salt and sugar to taste. Simmer slowly for 3 to 4 minutes, till heated through, but not cooked too dry. Add margarine.

## Peggy's Coleslaw

*serves 8*

1/2 medium head green cabbage, shredded
1/2 medium head red cabbage, shredded
1 stalk celery, chopped
2 medium carrots, shredded

**Dressing**
1/2 cup light mayonnaise
1/2 cup ranch dressing
1 teaspoon (or to taste) salt
1/4 cup sugar
3 tablespoons (or to taste) lemon juice or vinegar

| PER SERVING | |
| --- | --- |
| CALORIES: | 147 |
| TOTAL FAT: | 11g |
| CHOLESTEROL: | 8mg |
| SODIUM: | 521mg |
| CARBOHYDRATE: | 12g |
| PROTEIN: | 1g |

Mix shredded cabbage with DRESSING; serve.

## Microwave Apple Crisp

*serves 6*

6 cups peeled, cored, and sliced apples
3 tablespoons orange juice
6 tablespoons margarine
3/4 cups brown sugar
3/4 cups quick oats
1/2 cup flour
1 teaspoon cinnamon
Sprinkle of nutmeg (optional)

| PER SERVING | |
|---|---|
| CALORIES: | 316 |
| TOTAL FAT: | 13g |
| CHOLESTEROL: | 0mg |
| SODIUM: | 141mg |
| CARBOHYDRATE: | 50g |
| PROTEIN: | 3g |

Place sliced apples in an 8" x 8" baking dish. Sprinkle with orange juice.

Melt margarine in a small mixing bowl on high power, 1 to 1 1/2 minutes. Stir in remaining ingredients until crumbly; spread over apples. Microwave on high 8 minutes. Rotate dish 1/2 turn; microwave 8 more minutes or until apples are tender. Serve cold or warm with whipped topping or ice cream.

## Lemonade With Lemonade Ice Cubes

*Peggy's hostess tip:* Lemonade was my Dad's specialty, made, of course, with fresh lemons, and not too sweet! I add lemonade to an ice-cube tray and place one of the lemonade ice cubes in each glass. This keeps the drink cool without diluting it.

# SABBATH DINNER MENU #38

*Contributed by Louise (Honey) Struck Speyer of Keene, Texas*

**Grapenuts Roast**

**Steamed carrots**

**Green baby lima beans**

**Baked potatoes**

**Mandarin Orange–Cottage Cheese Salad**

**Banana Pudding**

*Honey says:* When my two sisters, my brother, and I were growing up, Mother always made a lot of pies and cakes. But she made Banana Pudding most often. In our adult years, we still make a lot of Banana Pudding, and it is still one of our favorites.

Our sister Helen made the Grapenuts Roast and the other items on this menu many times. Grapenuts Roast was her very favorite. She loved to cook and was in the kitchen with our mother from an early age. My sister Anna Kent and I share these recipes in loving memory of our mother, Helen Struck, and our sister, Helen Murdock.

*Jackie says:* When we were fifteen years old, Honey and I were roommates in academy at Southwestern Junior College in Keene, Texas. Honey had it over all us girls because the boys could call across the campus, "Hi, Honey!" and the faculty couldn't do anything about it, because that was the name her family, the church friends, and everyone, called her. I think her family nicknamed her that because she was always smiling and congenial—a special person. Our friendship has lasted through the years, and I am proud to have this menu from Honey and her sister Anna in our book. This is good ol' Texas cooking!

## Grapenuts Roast

*serves 8*

| PER SERVING | |
|---|---|
| CALORIES: | 128 |
| TOTAL FAT: | 11g |
| CHOLESTEROL: | 53mg |
| SODIUM: | 327mg |
| CARBOHYDRATE: | 6g |
| PROTEIN: | 4g |

1 1/2 cups Grapenuts® cereal
1 cup finely chopped celery
1 1/2 cups 2% milk
2 teaspoons butter
3/4 cup finely chopped pecans
1 teaspoon salt
2 eggs
1/2 cup finely chopped onion

Mix ingredients and put into a lightly greased 1 1/2 quart baking dish. Bake at 350°F for 30 to 40 minutes, or till done.

## Mandarin Orange- Cottage Cheese Salad

*serves 10*

| PER SERVING | |
|---|---|
| CALORIES: | 261 |
| TOTAL FAT: | 13g |
| CHOLESTEROL: | 3mg |
| SODIUM: | 326mg |
| CARBOHYDRATE: | 24g |
| PROTEIN: | 10g |

1 24-ounce container small-curd
   cottage cheese
1 12-ounce container light
   whipped topping
1 3-ounce package orange gelatin
2 8-ounce cans mandarin oranges
   (drain 1 can only)
1 cup pecan pieces (optional)

Combine all ingredients, mix well; chill till serving time.

## Banana Pudding

*serves 8*

1 1/4 cups 2% milk
1 6-ounce box vanilla instant pudding mix
1 14-ounce can sweetened condensed milk
1 8-ounce container whipped topping
Vanilla wafers (enough to cover bottom and sides of dish)
2 bananas

| PER SERVING | |
|---|---|
| CALORIES: | 461 |
| TOTAL FAT: | 14g |
| CHOLESTEROL: | 20mg |
| SODIUM: | 467mg |
| CARBOHYDRATE: | 77g |
| PROTEIN: | 6g |

Mix milk, pudding mix, and condensed milk together; stir by hand about 3 to 4 minutes, until well blended. Fold in whipped topping. Let set for 3 to 5 minutes. Line a glass serving bowl with vanilla wafers. Slice bananas over wafers; pour pudding over bananas. *Can top with small amount of whipped topping when ready to serve. Let guests serve themselves.*

**Carol's Sweet-and-Sour
Meatballs**

**Jicama, Avocado, and Grapefruit
Salad**

**Vegetable of choice**

**Whole-wheat dinner rolls**

**Lickety-Split Apricot Whip**

# SABBATH DINNER MENU #39

*Contributed by Ruth Sipkens of Yuma, Arizona*

*Jackie says:* Ruth and John have been special friends since we first met in 1962, in Ceylon (now Sri Lanka). In 1986, we again served overseas together, in the Far Eastern Division, living in Manila, Philippines. We've always enjoyed Ruth's Sabbath dinners.

*Ruth says:* This Sweet-and-Sour Meatballs recipe is one of my favorite entrees. It's also good as a covered dish for potlucks or patio suppers. The entree can be served with its sweet-and-sour sauce, as is, or over rice. Or, use the browned meatballs with spaghetti sauce.

Because the entree is rich, I like to serve a light salad, such as Jicama, Avocado, and Grapefruit Salad. I hope you enjoy it as much as we do.

## Carol's Sweet-and-Sour Meatballs

*makes 45 meatballs*

1 20-ounce can Worthington® *Vegetarian Burger*®
1 1/4 cups Italian seasoned breadcrumbs
3 eggs, well beaten
    or 3/4 cup Morningstar Farms® *Scramblers*®
1 1/4 cups grated cheese
1 cup crushed Ritz® round crackers
2 tablespoons olive oil
Sweet-and-Sour Sauce (recipe follows)

Mix all ingredients to make firm meatballs. *Add more cracker crumbs if needed.* Add olive oil to a nonstick skillet; brown. Place in a 9" x 13" casserole dish. *If making a day ahead:* Cover and refrigerate.

*Ruth says:* When in a hurry, Carol has made these meatballs without browning; she said they turned out OK.

*When ready to bake:* Pour Sweet-and-Sour Sauce over meatballs. Bake, uncovered, at 350°F for 20 to 30 minutes (longer if meatballs are still cold from the refrigerator).

## Sweet-and-Sour Sauce

1 cup catsup
1 cup water
1/2 cup brown sugar
1 cup chili sauce
1/4 cup vinegar or lemon juice

| PER SERVING | |
|---|---|
| CALORIES: | 71 |
| TOTAL FAT: | 3g |
| CHOLESTEROL: | 16mg |
| SODIUM: | 237mg |
| CARBOHYDRATE: | 8g |
| PROTEIN: | 4g |

## Jicama, Avocado, and Grapefruit Salad

*serves 8*

4 cups mixed crisp salad greens
1 large ruby red grapefruit, peeled, membrane and seeds removed,
     and cut into $3/4$-inch cubes
1 large, firm avocado, peeled and cut into $3/4$-inch cubes
$1/2$ small- to medium-size jícama, peeled and cut into $1/2$-inch cubes

**Dressing**
$1/4$ cup nonfat or low-fat sour cream
2 tablespoons olive oil
2 tablespoons lime juice
1 tablespoon orange juice
$1 1/2$ teaspoon sugar or $1 1/2$ packets sugar substitute
$1/2$ teaspoon poppy seeds
$1/4$ teaspoon salt
3 drops of liquid red pepper seasoning (optional)

SALAD: Mix all ingredients together.

DRESSING: Whisk ingredients together, or use your favorite citrus dressing.

| PER SERVING | |
| --- | --- |
| CALORIES: | 111 |
| TOTAL FAT: | 7g |
| CHOLESTEROL: | 1mg |
| SODIUM: | 80mg |
| CARBOHYDRATE: | 11g |
| PROTEIN: | 2g |

## Lickety-Split Apricot Whip

*serves 6*

2 17-ounce cans apricots in syrup
   (reserve syrup)
1/4 cup sugar
1/8 teaspoon salt
1 cup heavy whipping cream
Rum flavoring (optional)

**Sauce**
Reserved syrup from apricots
1/2 cup sugar

| PER SERVING | |
|---|---|
| CALORIES: | 367 |
| TOTAL FAT: | 15g |
| CHOLESTEROL: | 54mg |
| SODIUM: | 77mg |
| CARBOHYDRATE: | 61g |
| PROTEIN: | 2g |

Purée apricots in a blender or food processor, with sugar, salt, and rum flavoring, if desired. Whip cream to stiff peaks; fold in apricot purée. Pour into a 9" x 9" metal pan; freeze for 2 hours.

SAUCE: Combine reserved syrup and sugar in a large saucepan. Boil over medium-high heat 10 to 12 minutes, until reduced to 1 cup. *While cooking, watch and stir so as not to scorch this sweetened syrup.* Remove from heat; cool.

Spoon frozen whip into dessert bowls. Top with sauce.

**Secret Spaghetti Sauce**
   *with hot spaghetti*

**Steamed broccoli**

**Tossed salad**

**French bread**

**Ice cream and wafer cookies**

# Sabbath Dinner Menu #40

*Contributed by Nancy Beck Irland of Hillsboro, Oregon*

*Nancy says:* The legend from my husband Gary's family is that this recipe was obtained by a relative who was a waitress in an exclusive Italian restaurant in New York, many, many years ago. She asked the chef for the spaghetti-sauce recipe, but he wouldn't give it to her. However, he had it taped to the corner of his worktable. Each time she passed that corner, she wrote down one more ingredient, until she had the entire recipe for her family.

It is such an easy recipe, I can believe the story could be true. And the sauce only gets better the longer it simmers. My family has now made a tradition of having this special sauce whenever someone comes home from college, on Christmas Eve, and any other special occasion—or just whenever we feel like it. It freezes well and makes enough for about 4 or 5 meals.

For many years, this was my secret recipe, shared with only a select few. However, my family claims that, no matter who else makes the sauce, I must still have some secret, because theirs never tastes like mine. With that caveat, I now have permission to share the secret recipe.

*Jackie says:* Our daughter Nancy is right! I have her recipe, and when I make it, it is never quite the same as hers, but it is delicious, anyway. And we like to simmer vegetarian meatballs in it for about 20 minutes before serving. I put the spaghetti on the platter, line the meatballs all around the spaghetti, spoon some of the sauce on top, and garnish with a sprig of parsley. Pass the remaining sauce. Yum!

## Secret Spaghetti Sauce

*makes 15 cups*

| PER SERVING | |
|---|---|
| CALORIES: | 118 |
| TOTAL FAT: | 9g |
| CHOLESTEROL: | 0mg |
| SODIUM: | 551mg |
| CARBOHYDRATE: | 10g |
| PROTEIN: | 2g |

1 cup olive oil
1/4 cup margarine
3 medium onions, chopped
3 cloves garlic, chopped
1 teaspoon ground oregano (you can add a teaspoon of oregano leaves, if you wish)
3 bay leaves

1 tablespoon salt
1 tablespoon sugar
2 32-ounce cans whole or recipe-ready canned tomatoes
5 6-ounce cans tomato paste (or equivalent)
1/4 to 1/2 teaspoon Tabasco® sauce
1 to 2 cups water

Sauté onions and garlic in oil and margarine until caramelized. Add oregano, bay leaves, salt, and sugar; simmer for 2 to 3 minutes, stirring frequently. Add tomatoes, tomato paste, Tabasco® sauce *(the secret ingredient!),* and 1 cup of water. Stir well; simmer with the lid on, for 2 hours, stirring as needed. *Can add more water if necessary. Can also add canned mushrooms if desired, or fresh mushrooms, sliced and browned in a skillet. The sauce can be made a week ahead and kept in the refrigerator or freezer.*

*Nancy says:* When you get home after church, cook enough spaghetti for the number of people you are serving. Turn on the oven to 350°F for the bread, make the salad, steam the broccoli, and heat the sauce. Slice the loaf of French bread and then put it into a paper grocery sack, wrapping the sack around the bread, to hold the slices together. Run water over the sack for just a second, and put the moistened sack into the oven for about 15 minutes. The bread will be steamed on the inside and crunchy on the outside. Delicious served with room-temperature butter.

# SABBATH DINNER MENU #41

*Contributed by LaVerne Northrup of Loma Linda, California*

*Jackie says:* I met LaVerne after she was married to Bob, with whom I had gone to Sabbath School when we were twelve years old. Bob's mother, Mrs. Mae Northrup, was my junior Sabbath School teacher and one of the first Sabbath School teachers I remember. She was so kind and patient, and I just loved her from the start. My mother and I had just moved to Texas, and were new to everyone there in the Dallas Church. Mrs. Northrup had told me she lived in the same area of Dallas where we were living. Mother was a single parent, and we didn't have much money. One Sabbath the call was made for a Week of Sacrifice offering, and my mother put all she had in the offering plate. After church, she admitted that she didn't have enough streetcar fare to take us home. I saw Mrs. Northrup and her family going to the parking lot, so I quickly ran to her and asked if my mother and I could ride with her. She quickly said, "Why, yes, of course you may! We'd be happy to have you!" My mother was, of course, embarrassed, but we made new friends, and I never forgot sweet Mrs. Northrup. She was a very positive influence in my young life.

**Cream-Cheese Patties**

**Potato Slabs**

**Cooked Carrots**

**Pea and Celery Salad**

**Fresh Strawberry Pie**

*LaVerne says:* These Cream-Cheese Patties were a favorite of my late mother-in-law, Mae Northrup. She was a marvelous cook. The Pea and Celery Salad is my husband's second-favorite salad!

## Cream-Cheese Patties

*serves 8*

6 eggs or 1 ¹/₂ cups Morningstar Farms® *Scramblers*®
1 8-ounce package low-fat cream cheese, at room temperature
1 ¹/₂ cups saltine cracker crumbs
1 cup chopped pecans or walnuts
¹/₂ teaspoon (or to taste) salt
1 10.75-ounce can low-fat condensed cream of mushroom soup, diluted with a half can water
    or 1 10.75-ounce can condensed cream of tomato soup, diluted with a half can water

| PER SERVING | |
| --- | --- |
| CALORIES: | 318 |
| TOTAL FAT: | 20g |
| CHOLESTEROL: | 156mg |
| SODIUM: | 630mg |
| CARBOHYDRATE: | 25g |
| PROTEIN: | 11g |

Mix eggs and cream cheese thoroughly. Add cracker crumbs, chopped nuts, and salt. Drop from tablespoon into a medium-hot skillet coated with oil. Brown quickly; place into a baking dish. Cover patties *(or loaf: See below)* with half-diluted mushroom or tomato soup. Bake at 350°F for 45 minutes.

*Options:* Diced onion and/or celery can be added to the patties or sauce. Mixture can be made into a loaf by placing it into a greased baking dish.

## Potato Slabs

serves 8

8 medium potatoes, boiled in the skin
Salt to taste

Leave peelings on cold, boiled potatoes; slice into 1/2-inch widths. Heat until browned in an iron skillet that has been brushed with oil. Sprinkle salt on each side as they are heating. Serve on a platter with sprigs of parsley or radish slices.

## Pea and Celery Salad

serves 8

1 can green peas, drained (frozen peas do not taste right for this salad)
1 large stalk celery, cut to 1/4-inch slices
1 tablespoon finely chopped onion
2 tablespoons light mayonnaise
2 tablespoons lemon juice
1/4 teaspoon salt

| PER SERVING | |
|---|---|
| CALORIES: | 41 |
| TOTAL FAT: | 1g |
| CHOLESTEROL: | 1mg |
| SODIUM: | 227mg |
| CARBOHYDRATE: | 7g |
| PROTEIN: | 2g |

Combine all ingredients; mix thoroughly. Refrigerate. *Can be served the same day or later.*

## Fresh Strawberry Pie

*serves 8*

1 12-ounce can frozen apple juice
3 tablespoons cornstarch
1/2 cup water
1/2 teaspoon vanilla
Dash of salt
3 cups sliced fresh strawberries
Prepared graham-cracker crust
1 8-ounce container light whipped topping

| PER SERVING | |
|---|---|
| CALORIES: | 320 |
| TOTAL FAT: | 11g |
| CHOLESTEROL: | 0mg |
| SODIUM: | 203mg |
| CARBOHYDRATE: | 51g |
| PROTEIN: | 2g |

Bring undiluted apple juice to a boil. Mix cornstarch in water with salt; pour into apple juice while stirring. Continue to stir over medium heat until mixture thickens. Remove from heat; add vanilla. Refrigerate overnight.

Make or purchase a graham-cracker crust. Add strawberries to the apple juice mixture; pour into the pie crust. Set in the freezer while eating dinner. *Whipped topping may be added before or after freezer cooling.*

# Sabbath Dinner Menu #42

*Contributed by Eva Remboldt of Boring, Oregon*

*Jackie says:* Eva was my mentor when we lived in Spokane, Washington. She was a great hostess, loved to work outside, and she and Reuben had the most beautiful yard in the community. She always knew the answers to my questions—how to remove a stain or whatever. We have been friends through the years, and though she now cooks less than she used to, she has shared one of her favorite menus with us.

Rice "Plus" Casserole

Microwaved Broccoli

Relish Platter

Whole-wheat rolls

Creamy Apricot Pie

## Rice "Plus" Casserole

*serves 10*

1/2 cube (1/4 cup) margarine
2 cups chopped onion
2 cups sliced celery
1/2 cup diced green bell pepper
1/2 cup diced red bell pepper
3 teaspoons seasoning salt
4 teaspoons chickenlike seasoning and broth mix

1 cup mixed nuts (cashews, walnuts, and Brazil nuts), coarsely chopped
4 cups cooked rice (flavor water with 1 tablespoon chickenlike seasoning and broth mix)
1 cup grated Longhorn cheese or Cheddar-flavor soy cheese

| PER SERVING | |
| --- | --- |
| CALORIES: | 297 |
| TOTAL FAT: | 17g |
| CHOLESTEROL: | 12mg |
| SODIUM: | 818mg |
| CARBOHYDRATE: | 30g |
| PROTEIN: | 8g |

Sauté onion, celery, and pepper in margarine. *Do not cover the skillet, as the vegetables will lose their color.* Add seasonings; stir in nuts and rice. Pour into a 9" x 13" casserole. Cover and refrigerate.

*Sabbath morning:* When ready to bake, sprinkle cheese over the top. Bake in a 350°F oven until cheese melts and casserole is hot.

## Microwaved Broccoli

Cut broccoli into florets; place in a flat microwave-safe dish with 2 tablespoons water. Cover with plastic wrap; put in microwave. Cook for 3 to 4 minutes, or until tender but still bright green. Serve immediately.

## Relish Platter

Arrange lettuce leaves on salad platter; top with an arrangement of halved small Roma tomatoes, cucumber slices, baby carrots, celery sticks, radishes, and olives. Garnish with parsley.

## Creamy Apricot Pie

*serves 8*

1 15-ounce can apricot halves in syrup, drained (reserve 1/2 cup syrup)
1 egg yolk
1 12-ounce can evaporated milk
1 3.4-ounce box vanilla cook-and-serve pudding
1 9-inch baked pie shell
2 teaspoons cornstarch
1 5.5-ounce can (2/3 cup) apricot nectar
1/4 cup sliced almonds, toasted

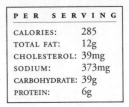

| PER SERVING | |
|---|---|
| CALORIES: | 285 |
| TOTAL FAT: | 12g |
| CHOLESTEROL: | 39mg |
| SODIUM: | 373mg |
| CARBOHYDRATE: | 39g |
| PROTEIN: | 6g |

Set apricots aside. Mix egg yolk, milk, and reserved syrup; stir in pudding mix till smooth. Bring to a boil over medium heat; stir until thickened. Chop 1/2 cup apricots; add to pudding. Pour into baked pie shell; refrigerate.

GLAZE: Combine cornstarch and apricot nectar till smooth. Boil 2 minutes, until thick.

Cut remaining apricots into thirds; arrange over pie filling. Spoon glaze over the top. Sprinkle with toasted almonds. Chill till time to serve.

**Barbequed Meatballs (Vegan)**

**Onion-Mix Potatoes**

*Spinach-mandarin salad*

*Relish platter*

*Whole-wheat rolls*

**Danish Strawberry Pie**

# SABBATH DINNER MENU #43

*Contributed by Linda Foerderer of College Place, Washington*

*Sabbath preparation:* Both the meatballs and sauce can be made a couple of days in advance. On Sabbath morning, put meatballs in a baking dish. Pour barbeque sauce over the meatballs, cover, and place in oven. Set timer to bake for 60 minutes.

Pour the potatoes into a baking dish, cover, and place in the oven for 60 minutes, along with the meatballs.

## Barbequed Meatballs (Vegan)

*makes 58 balls*

1 20-ounce can Worthington®
    *Low-fat Vegetarian Burger*®
9 eggs or 2 1/4 cups Morningstar Farms®
    *Scramblers*®
2 cups Italian seasoned breadcrumbs

1/2 teaspoon garlic powder
2 teaspoons onion powder
2 cups grated Cheddar-flavor soy cheese
Barbeque Sauce (recipe follows—can also use
    Quick Barbeque Sauce or other favorite)

Mix well (except for sauce), cover, and place in the refrigerator for at least 2 hours. Preheat the oven to 350°F. Spoon the mixture onto a greased cookie sheet. *(I roll them by hand into walnut-size balls.) They are very sticky.* Bake for 20 minutes. Remove from the cookie sheet; place on a cooling rack. When cooled, place in a bag in the refrigerator.

*When ready to serve:* Pour Barbeque Sauce over meatballs in a casserole; bake at 350°F for 45 minutes.

## Barbeque Sauce

1/4 cup olive oil
1 onion, chopped
1 cup ketchup
1 teaspoon salt

1/2 cup brown sugar
1 teaspoon cumin powder
1/2 teaspoon liquid smoke
3 cups tomato juice

Sauté onion in olive oil. Add ketchup, salt, brown sugar, cumin, and liquid smoke. Simmer for a few minutes before adding tomato juice. Cook over low heat for 45 to 60 minutes. Let cool, put into a jar, and refrigerate.

| PER SERVING | |
|---|---|
| CALORIES: | 71 |
| TOTAL FAT: | 3g |
| CHOLESTEROL: | >1mg |
| SODIUM: | 365mg |
| CARBOHYDRATE: | 7g |
| PROTEIN: | 5g |

## Quick Barbeque Sauce

*Linda says:* My daughter and her friends like this quick-to-prepare sauce better than the other one. They say it has more flavor. You can also use your favorite barbeque sauce.

1 cup barbeque sauce
1 cup honey
1 cup ketchup

## Onion-Mix Potatoes

*serves 8*

6 large red potatoes, washed, dried, and diced
1 package onion mushroom soup mix
2 tablespoons olive oil (may need a bit more)

| PER SERVING | |
|---|---|
| CALORIES: | 89 |
| TOTAL FAT: | 4g |
| CHOLESTEROL: | >1mg |
| SODIUM: | 440mg |
| CARBOHYDRATE: | 13g |
| PROTEIN: | 2g |

Put ingredients into a self-sealing bag; zip the bag shut. Work the bag with your hands until the potatoes are covered with the mix. Pour potatoes into a baking dish; cover. *Can keep in the refrigerator overnight.* Bake, covered, at 350°F for 45 to 60 minutes.

## Danish Strawberry Pie

*serves 8*

1 9-inch graham cracker crust
2 pints fresh strawberries, washed and hulled
1/4 cup sugar
1 package strawberry-flavor Danish Dessert® pudding and pie filling
1 8-ounce container light whipped topping

| PER SERVING | |
| --- | --- |
| CALORIES: | 264 |
| TOTAL FAT: | 8g |
| CHOLESTEROL: | 0mg |
| SODIUM: | 171mg |
| CARBOHYDRATE: | 47g |
| PROTEIN: | 2g |

Slice 1 pint strawberries; place in pie crust. Crush remaining strawberries; sweeten with sugar. Add Danish Dessert®; bring to a boil. Pour over strawberries in the pie crust. Place in the refrigerator; add whipped topping when ready to serve.

**Italian Meatballs**

**Scalloped potatoes**

**Caesar salad**

**Corn**

**Frozen Cookies 'n Cream Pie**

# SABBATH DINNER MENU #44

*Contributed by Marilyn Weststrate Lisk of Oshawa, Ontario, Canada*

*Jackie says:* When I was secretary to the president of Kingsway College, Marilyn was one of my student secretaries. Some months ago—about twenty years after we had worked together—Marilyn phoned and said, "Guess what! I have your old job, and, believe it or not, many procedures are still done much the same way as we used to do them, so I can just step right in. And, the minutes we typed are in the archives; it has been fun seeing them again." I am so happy to be back in touch with Marilyn, and I know you will enjoy her recipes.

*Marilyn says:* My husband Cameron and I have two sons, Kyle and Colton. Our boys enjoy Sabbath dinner together as a family but enjoy it more if we invite friends or family to join us. They like that we set the table with our good china and crystal glasses. Colton loves to have candles on the table, so we do that occasionally. The recipes I've given are all family favorites!

I try to plan ahead for this meal, so that I do very little on Sabbath. The meatballs are placed in the refrigerator on Friday, or even frozen a week before! I set them out on the counter before I leave for church and add the sauce. I place them in the 350° F oven as soon as I get home from church. The scalloped potatoes are placed in the refrigerator on Friday and ready to be placed into a timed oven on Sabbath. The frozen dessert can be made up to a week before and kept covered in the freezer.

## Italian Meatballs

*serves 8*

| PER SERVING | |
| --- | --- |
| CALORIES: | 184 |
| TOTAL FAT: | 6g |
| CHOLESTEROL: | 72mg |
| SODIUM: | 317mg |
| CARBOHYDRATE: | 25g |
| PROTEIN: | 7g |

**Meatballs**
1/2 cup low-fat Cheddar cheese, shredded
1/2 cup pecan (or other nut) meal
3 eggs or 3/4 cup Morningstar Farms® *Scramblers*®
1/2 cup minced onion
1 1/2 cups salted cracker crumbs
1 clove fresh garlic, minced

**Sauce**
1 8-ounce can tomato soup
1/4 cup ketchup
1/4 cup water
Pinch of cumin powder

Combine all MEATBALL ingredients; mix well. Form into small balls; pan-fry using nonstick spray or olive oil until balls are just set. Place fried meatballs on a paper towel to absorb oil, then place into a baking dish. Cover meatballs with SAUCE; bake, uncovered, at 350°F for 30 minutes.

## Frozen Cookies 'n Cream Pie

*serves 10*

1 1/4 cups chocolate cookie crumbs
1/4 cup granulated sugar
1/4 cup low-fat margarine or butter, melted
1/2 gallon cookies 'n cream* ice cream, slightly softened
1 12-ounce jar chocolate fudge ice cream topping
1 8-ounce container light whipped topping

| PER SERVING | |
|---|---|
| CALORIES: | 457 |
| TOTAL FAT: | 23g |
| CHOLESTEROL: | 48mg |
| SODIUM: | 358mg |
| CARBOHYDRATE: | 62g |
| PROTEIN: | 6g |

In a medium bowl mix cookie crumbs, sugar, and melted margarine. Press into a 9-inch springform pan; chill in the freezer. Remove pan from the freezer; spread ice cream evenly over the crust. Return pan to freezer; let set until hard. When it is time for dessert, remove pan from the freezer; cover ice cream with chocolate topping (use all the topping). Remove the springform; garnish with whipped topping.

*Any flavor ice cream can be used.*

# SABBATH DINNER MENU #45

*Contributed by Evelyn Smith of Stone Mountain, Georgia*

*Jackie says:* Evelyn is my "little" cousin, eight years younger than I. I used to take her for rides on my bike and have birthday parties for her. She was the closest thing to a little sister I ever had. Unfortunately, we have been separated half a world apart for many of the past years, but always kept in touch on birthdays and Christmas. I asked her to share one of her favorite tuna recipes with me, and I have substituted Worthington® *Tuno*® for the flaked tuna fish in the original recipe. This entire menu is delicious! Ed and I couldn't get enough of the spoonbread and actually preferred white cornmeal.

*Evelyn says:* What fun to be asked to send a recipe! The Mock Tuna Balls go well with the Herbed Spinach Bake. It is the one the children enjoyed, so we had it often. Mother's Spoonbread was a recipe of my mother's, and it is heavenly. It makes me hungry and a little weepy to think of how many times she fixed this for us. Hope you will enjoy it as much as our family has.

**Mock Tuna Balls**

**Herbed Spinach Bake**

**Tossed salad**

**Mother's Spoonbread**

*Ice cream and cookies*

## Mock Tuna Balls

*makes 36 balls*

1 12-ounce package Worthington® *Tuno®*, drained in a colander
1 1/3 cups very dry (no milk or potato water) mashed potatoes
12 pimento-stuffed green olives, chopped
16 capers, chopped
2 cloves garlic, minced or pressed
2 tablespoons minced fresh or 1 tablespoon dried parsley
2 teaspoons dried basil
1 cup Italian seasoned breadcrumbs
1/2 cup olive oil
3/4 cup pecan meal (optional)

Press out as much liquid as possible from the *Tuno®* as it drains. Mash potatoes just until most of the lumps are out. Combine *Tuno®*, mashed potatoes, olives, capers, garlic, parsley, basil, and breadcrumbs. Form into walnut-size balls. Over medium heat, fry the balls on all sides until light brown (4 to 5 minutes). *(Using two spoons to turn the balls is helpful.)* Remove from oil; roll in pecan meal.

*To serve:* Place *Tuno®* balls on a platter. Garnish with parsley sprigs.

*Note: These* Tuno® *balls freeze well. If they have been fried before freezing, just heat in the oven at 350° F for 20 to 30 minutes. If frozen before frying, defrost and proceed as directed in the recipe.*

| PER SERVING | |
| --- | --- |
| CALORIES: | 58 |
| TOTAL FAT: | 8g |
| CHOLESTEROL: | 0mg |
| SODIUM: | 211mg |
| CARBOHYDRATE: | 2g |
| PROTEIN: | 1g |

## Herbed Spinach Bake

*serves 6*

1 10-ounce package frozen chopped
    spinach, cooked and drained
1 cup cooked rice
1 cup shredded sharp
    processed cheese
2 eggs, slightly beaten or 1/2 cup
    Morningstar Farms® Scramblers®

2 tablespoons soft butter
1/3 cup 2% milk
2 tablespoons chopped onion
1/2 teaspoon Worcestershire sauce
1 teaspoon salt
1/4 teaspoon crushed rosemary
    or thyme

| PER SERVING | |
| --- | --- |
| CALORIES: | 148 |
| TOTAL FAT: | 7g |
| CHOLESTEROL: | 67mg |
| SODIUM: | 587mg |
| CARBOHYDRATE: | 12g |
| PROTEIN: | 9g |

Combine all ingredients; pour into a well-greased 10" x 6" x 2" loaf pan. Bake at 350°F for 20 to 25 minutes, until knife inserted in the center comes out clean. Cut into squares; serve.

## Mother's Spoonbread

*serves 6*

1 cup cornmeal
1 1/2 teaspoons salt
1 cup cold milk
2 cups hot milk

2 eggs
3 tablespoons melted shortening
    or oil

| PER SERVING | |
| --- | --- |
| CALORIES: | 227 |
| TOTAL FAT: | 11g |
| CHOLESTEROL: | 71mg |
| SODIUM: | 613mg |
| CARBOHYDRATE: | 24g |
| PROTEIN: | 8g |

Mix cornmeal and salt; add to cold milk. Stir until smooth; add to hot milk. Cook until thickened (about 5 minutes), stirring constantly. Beat eggs, add small amount of the cooked mixture, and blend. Stir in remaining cooked mixture and oil. Pour into a well-greased 1 1/2 quart casserole; bake at 350°F about 50 minutes until done, or until it is slightly browned on top and puffy. Serve immediately, topped with melted butter, to six happy souls!

**Vegetable *Biriyani***

**FriChik Curry**

**Tomato and Cucumber
Yogurt Salad *(Raita)***

**Vermicelli Pudding *(Payasam)***

# SABBATH DINNER MENU #46

*Contributed by Mrs. Ammini Samuel and Jennifer Samuel
of Silver Spring, Maryland, and Kayenta, Arizona*

*Kristi says:* Jenny and I went to school together from fourth grade at John Nevins Andrews Elementary, where we sat next to each other in treble choir. Through college at Andrews University, we were just two rooms down the hall from each other in the girls' dorm. It is so special to have a good friend who shares so many of the same memories.

When we were little girls, we loved to go to Jenny's house for slumber parties because Mrs. Samuel would make us chocolate chip pancakes in the morning! Over the years we have had lots of meals around their table, every one delicious. Of course, we especially love it when she cooks Indian food for us, and so I'm thrilled that she and Jenny have put together this Sabbath dinner menu of rice and curry.

## Vegetable Biriyani

*serves 8*

| PER SERVING | |
|---|---|
| CALORIES: | 293 |
| TOTAL FAT: | 5g |
| CHOLESTEROL: | 0mg |
| SODIUM: | 328mg |
| CARBOHYDRATE: | 53g |
| PROTEIN: | 10g |

2 cups uncooked basmati rice
2 tablespoons vegetable oil
1 onion, chopped
6 cloves garlic, minced
1 cup chopped cilantro leaves
1 inch fresh ginger, peeled and minced
1 cup sliced carrots
1 cup frozen peas

1 cup cut green beans
1 cup lima beans
1 tablespoon ground fennel seed
1/4 teaspoon ground cardamom
1/4 teaspoon ground cloves
2 teaspoons salt
4 cups boiling water

Soak rice, drain, and set aside for about 10 minutes. Sauté onion, garlic, cilantro, and ginger in vegetable oil until onion is tender. Add carrots, peas, and beans to onion mixture. Cook for 5 minutes. Add rice to vegetable mix. Add fennel seed, cardamom, cloves, and salt. Add water; bring to a boil. Cook until water is level with rice. Cover; reduce heat to very low. Cook until rice is tender. Remove from heat; let stand for 10 minutes. Stir mixture with a fork.

## FriChik Curry

*serves 6*

1 tablespoon oil
1 large onion, chopped
3 cloves garlic, minced
3 Roma tomatoes, chopped
2 tablespoons ground coriander
2 teaspoons ground red pepper
1 to 2 tablespoons ground fennel seed

1 teaspoon salt
3 red potatoes, cubed small
2 cups water
1 12-ounce can Worthington®
    FriChik®, cubed
    or Worthington® Diced Chik®

| PER SERVING | |
|---|---|
| CALORIES: | 102 |
| TOTAL FAT: | 4g |
| CHOLESTEROL: | 0mg |
| SODIUM: | 543mg |
| CARBOHYDRATE: | 12g |
| PROTEIN: | 6g |

Sauté onion and garlic in oil until tender. Add tomatoes, coriander, red pepper, fennel seed, and salt. Add potatoes and water. Cook for 10 to 15 minutes until potatoes are tender. Add *FriChik®*; cook until curry is thick.

## Tomato and Cucumber Yogurt Salad (Raita)

*serves 8*

2 medium tomatoes, chopped
1 cucumber, chopped
1 small onion, chopped (red onion is pretty)
16 ounces plain nonfat yogurt
2 tablespoons chopped coriander leaves

| PER SERVING | |
|---|---|
| CALORIES: | 48 |
| TOTAL FAT: | >1g |
| CHOLESTEROL: | 1mg |
| SODIUM: | 47mg |
| CARBOHYDRATE: | 8g |
| PROTEIN: | 4g |

Mix all ingredients together. Add salt to taste.

## Vermicelli Pudding (Payasam)

*serves 8*

2 tablespoons butter
8 ounces vermicelli noodles
5 cups milk
2 cups water
1 cup sugar
1/2 cup chopped nuts
1 cup raisins
1/2 teaspoon cardamom
Pinch of salt
1/2 can (14 to 16 ounces) coconut milk

| PER SERVING | |
|---|---|
| CALORIES: | 468 |
| TOTAL FAT: | 17g |
| CHOLESTEROL: | 19mg |
| SODIUM: | 117mg |
| CARBOHYDRATE: | 75g |
| PROTEIN: | 8g |

Sauté vermicelli noodles in butter until golden brown. Boil milk and water; add sugar and noodles. Cook for 5 minutes. *Do not overcook noodles.* Sauté nuts and raisins in butter until raisins puff up; add to noodle mixture. Add cardamom, salt, and coconut milk. Stir and serve.

## WORTHINGTON® FOOD INDEX